IRISH BLOOD

DENNIS J. CLARK

IRISH BLOOD

Northern Ireland
and the American Conscience

National University Publications
KENNIKAT PRESS   //   1977
Port Washington, N. Y.   //   London

Manufactured in the United States of America

Published by
Kennikat Press Corp.
Port Washington, N. Y./London

Library of Congress Cataloging in Publication Data

Clark, Dennis, 1927–
    Irish blood.

    Bibliography: p.
    Includes index.
    1. Northern Ireland—History—1969–
2. Irish Americans. I. Title.
DA990.U46C54   941.6'082'4   76-21808
ISBN 0-8046-9163-0

To my children:
Conna, Brendan, Padraig, Ciaran, Brian, Brigid,
so that they might study Ireland
and care for its future.

CONTENTS

PREFACE

In the world of turbulence, insurgency, and political crisis that has chal-
lenged mankind's hopes for peace in recent years, Ireland has once again
suffered that violent disruption so common in her history. Like many people with strong ties to Ireland, I have been especially grieved since 1969 by
the Ulster tragedy. I was in Belfast in 1969 when the barricades were first
thrown up amid rioting and hysteria. My work with violent race relations
situations in various American communities made me sensible of the cruel-
ties that riot conditions entail. In subsequent visits to Northern Ireland my
worst fears have been borne out. Within this last year I have witnessed the
bomb tremors and destruction that have so changed the ancient religious
seat of the town of Armagh in which two huge Cathedrals testify to the
ideals of brotherhood. Some of my friends in Northern Ireland have suffered
terribly from the intimidation and dislocation caused by the violence. A
man with whom I shared an evening in an American university trying to
interpret the breakdown in Northern Ireland was later shot dead on a street
in Belfast. My address to the Ulster tragedy is one that shares the pain and
distress of that deranged situation.

Whatever road out of turmoil is found for Northern Ireland, it will not
be found by leaders who specialize in slogans and cheap harangues. It can
only be found through reasoned searching, the growth of trust, and an
enlarged understanding of political and human rights. The English and Irish
partisans of rigid and arrogant positions about Northern Ireland deserve
the eternal contempt of every humane person who has witnessed the bloody
sacrifices offered to political and religious bigotry in Ulster in our time.

This book is an attempt to produce some enlargement of understanding
about one feature of the Northern Ireland problem, its relation to the United

States and to Irish-Americans. It is, I believe, an accurate record of important activities in the United States bearing on Northern Ireland. I have not refrained from trying to interpret many of these activities, for events without interpretation are threats to us all.

When Eamon de Valera visited the United States in 1919–1920 as a young revolutionary to rally support for the infant independent Irish state, the Irish in America were in some disarray. Factionalism was rife, largely deriving from the disparate ideas and political views of Irish-American leaders. The importance of this factionalism to students of Irish affairs is that it led to a protracted confusion about the nature of Irish-American efforts to aid Irish nationalist aspirations. For many years the best known book was Charles Callan Tansill's *America and the Fight for Irish Freedom* (New York: Devin-Adair Company, 1957). This version of Irish-American activities had wide influence. Yet, as later studies were to show, it was strongly biased in favor of one Irish-American faction. The result of this bias was that the crucial role of Americans in aiding one of the first liberation movements against colonialism of this century was not accurately presented. This defect, unfortunately, is part of a broader defect in historical scholarship in America that has traditionally misinterpreted or neglected the histories of many minority and ethnic groups.

In order to try to prevent a similar lapse with respect to Irish-American relations with the Northern Ireland problem since 1969, I have compiled in these pages what is largely a documentation of Irish-American activities concerning Ulster. That province of Ulster, historically broader than the present partitioned Six Counties, has had a disproportionate impact upon America. Its sons and daughters contributed much talent and democratic impulse to the frontier tradition in early America, and provided political, religious, and business leaders as our nation grew. We owe it to ourselves to try to understand the Ulster tragedy, for that tragedy is part of the strife of our times in this torn and bleeding world on the far side of the atomic epiphany.

Dennis Clark

IRISH BLOOD

1

THE OLD CAUSE

The Irish in America have ever been the heart's hope of those men in Ireland who have fought to assert their nationality against English domination. Since the days of the eighteenth-century Irish Volunteers, when Irish leaders looked with admiration on the deeds of the heroes of the American Revolution, the American connection has been a source of example and encouragement to those locked in struggle with Ireland's ancient foe. Theobold Wolfe Tone, inspired by the ideals of the French Revolution and burning with resentment against English injustice, visited the young American republic to see firsthand the wonders of its democracy. Daniel O'Connell, pursuing in the 1840s his scheme to sever Parliamentary ties between Ireland and England, found funds and supporters in the United States. In the period of the American Civil War, after the vast calamity of the potato famine had all but destroyed Irish political resistance, the Fenian Brotherhood in the United States masterminded plans for insurrection and guerrilla uprisings from its American refuge. In the great drive of Charles Stewart Parnell in the 1880s to obtain land reform, it was the American contributions to the Land League that advanced its power. The liberation movement that secured partial independence for Ireland in the 1920s called itself by the Gaelic title "Sinn Fein" ("Ourselves Alone"), but it too relied on the Irish in the United States for crucial support.[1]

It is not surprising, therefore, that in the late 1960s there emerged once again a cry from Ireland for aid from sons and daughters of Erin on the far side of the Atlantic. For all of the vaunted modernity that has supposedly transformed the world, some time-tested ties persist, and the reliance of Irish activists on supporters in America is one of these. When the long dormant problem of Northern Ireland erupted into civil disorders and violence in 1969, recourse to American assistance was sought not only because it was needed, but also because the American connection was traditional—almost habitual—and because it had indeed succeeded in bringing Irish nationalists succor in the past.

Irish nationalism has always had a high emotional content. Its history so often has been inundated by disaster that realism would have long ago condemned it. Emotional commitments, however, sustained it in the face of devastating reverses that could have wiped nationalism out as a force in Irish life. Interwoven with the emotion is the ideology of Irish nationalism which is a variant on the democratic republicanism that flowed from the watershed event of the French Revolution. In the last century this ideology, with its canons of egalitarianism, anti-imperialism and popular fulfillment through the nation state, found both practical expression and mystical inspiration through a succession of vivid and brilliant leaders. On both emotional and ideological grounds, the connection to America has been strong. The United States as the premier democratic republic of the modern world has served for generations as a model and an ideal for the nationalist. It has been a symbol and a practical demonstration that the dream of national independence and democratic government could be attained, and its existence has affirmed both hope and belief.[2]

When Irish nationalist fortunes were ground into bitter defeat, when England's sway seemed irreversible, when both popular opinion and sources of leadership seemed grimly poisoned by despair, America would still be there. The United States was a psychological refuge for the Irish nationalist smothered by English administration in his own country. It was a very special source of inspiration, not only because of its inherent qualities and novelty, but because from its founding Irishmen had gone to it and experienced its life. If kings and queens and dukes were held up to the Irish as worthy of veneration and allegiance, a letter from a relative in America would tell those in the old country that here, on this new continent, there were no such medieval figures, and that society flourished very nicely without them. If patriots were harried from the Irish shores, there was always hope that they could regroup and carry on their writing, teaching, and agitating from the shelter of the United States. Things were never so bad with the Irish nationalist that he could not draw some hope from the American quarter.

In the nineteenth-century age of mass emigration there was built up in the United States a complex nationalist redoubt for the benefit of Ireland. Immigrant memory, ethnic organizations, religious ties, and political experience combined to form a persistent, though unwieldy, web of nationalist sympathy and activity in America. The nineteenth century vogue for secret societies added a conspiratorial dimension to this immigrant establishment.[3]

English Parliamentarians would frequently expand
alarming potential of this overseas "empire of the b
find that the grudge the immigrants held her would
miseries for her as the strength of her imperial grasp
was more than emotion and ideology that were con
Irish redoubt. It was practical aid, strategic threat, a
as well.

A brief examination of the long Irish-American tr   ᴄᴛᴇᴅ ᴏʀ ɴationalist
effort in behalf of the old country should enable us to see that it has represented a number of important factors without which the agitator, whether
he be reformer or revolutionary, cannot effectively function.

Very early in the history of the United States, the tradition of political
refuge for opponents of English rule in Ireland was established. Indeed, a
number of prominent figures in the American revolutionary struggle against
England were men who had left Ireland because of the conditions of repression there. Commodore John Barry, Stephen Moylan, and others harbored venerable antagonisms toward English rule. Benjamin Franklin found
ready allies in Dublin when he visited there in behalf of American designs.
In 1798 there occurred a savage repression of a half-realized uprising in
Ireland, and Irish patriots were forced to flee their country in large numbers.
They found refuge in America, and from there continued their writings
and agitation against English interests.[4] Thus, there was established a tradition of Irish exile agitation from the earliest days of the republic. The
educated and articulate leaders of the liberal eighteenth-century activity
were followed by more humble men who in the nineteenth century were
driven from Ireland by chronic destitution and exploitation. The leaders
held a growing immigrant following on American shores, and this following
swelled to massive proportions as famine and destruction wracked Ireland
in the 1840s. In 1848 there was another abortive rising from which the
agitating conspirators had to flee. The ranks of the gifted exile agitators
were replenished by such men as Thomas Francis Meagher, Thomas D'Arcy
McGee and John Mitchel. Later, such fiery exponents of Irish nationalism
as John Boyle O'Reilly arrived in the United States after secretly being
liberated from Australian prison camps by Irish comrades operating from
America. All these took up the tradition of exile agitation. Indeed, John
Devoy, who was released from an English prison after the American Civil
War, came to New York and for more than sixty years made it his base for
a sustained and implacable career of revolutionary activity in the interests
of Irish independence.[5]

This tradition of refuge and revolutionary work carried into the twentieth century, and no less a figure than Eamon de Valera took part in it
when he eluded English authorities and was smuggled to the United States

...he future President of an independent Irish state helped to ...that state on American soil where he sought and found financial ...nd diplomatic recognition.[6] Dissenters in Irish politics, some of them ...ard core revolutionaries, continued to come to the United States even after Irish independence so that the tradition was sustained right into the late 1960s when the Provisional Irish Republican Army pitted itself against an English army equipped with the latest in sophisticated military technology.

The tradition of financial assistance to Irish political and revolutionary causes also has been a continued feature of the American connection with Ireland. Daniel O'Connell, the wily leader of Parliamentary campaigns for Irish causes, received much assistance for his drive to repeal the union of Irish legislative fortunes with England's Parliament in the 1840s. Even in the hungry forties of the last century money for famine relief was sent to Ireland by the refugees from hunger in America. Remittances for families and to Catholic parishes and institutions, such as the Catholic schools and universities, was steadily collected in America. In the second half of the nineteenth century the Fenian Brotherhood formed its own treasury to finance revolutionary work. The largest fund raising campaign of all, however, was that conducted in behalf of the Land League. The drive of Charles Stewart Parnell was to wrest land ownership from the exploitive class of absentee landlords and remand holdings to the tenant farmers whose lives depended upon the soil. Americans of many backgrounds contributed to Parnell's various funds, but the actual subscription network was composed of the immigrant Irish. Millions of dollars had flowed to Ireland, and it was the memory of the success of these fund raising efforts that brought de Valera to the United States in hopes of financing the Irish state born of the bitter fighting that had begun in 1916. It has been estimated that between 1848 and 1900 no less than $260 million American dollars flowed back to Ireland for various causes.[7]

If refuge and money were important to the Irish nationalists, military skills and arms were no less so. Pioneers in marshaling American talents in this respect were the leaders of the Fenian Brotherhood. This American-based society of agitators and conspirators took its form of organization from the European revolutionaries with whom its leaders, James Stephens and John O'Mahony, had taken refuge in Paris after the abortive rising of 1848. O'Mahony became the leader of the American Fenians and worked in close collaboration with the secret Irish Republican Brotherhood in Ireland.

It was the American Civil War, however, that endowed the Fenians with expert knowledge of the deadly arts of war. Young Irishmen by the thousands had served on both sides of the great conflict between the states. Some who had enlisted for the bounty in order to keep their families from hunger rose to posts of higher command. Units of the Irish Brigade had served in some of the fiercest fighting of the war.[8] From this background of struggle there emerged a phalanx of men with military knowledge and with a strong commitment to Irish liberation. They gravitated to the Fenian Brotherhood and concocted plans for a rising in Ireland in 1867. When this failed they actually mounted a small invasion of Canada to harass English administrators. They secured patents on the first practical submarine—to be used against English shipping—and undertook bomb plots against London's port facilities and bridges. They reached around the world to Australia to free imprisoned Irishmen. In 1866 and 1867 they sent more than 300 experienced military veterans to Ireland where they were to lead an uprising. The Fenian Brotherhood was talented, factious, furiously committed to its goals, and it kept alive a tradition of armed resistance against England when British power in Ireland was all but overwhelming.

In the nineteenth century there was still sufficient friction between the United States and England so that war between them was not out of the question. The Irish underground looked forward to such a conflict as an opportunity to send an expeditionary force to Ireland. There were numerous groups enlivened by the romantic military spirit of the age that could serve as the nucleus of such a force. One military training manual, written by Oliver O'Byrne and published in Boston as early as 1853, gave information on the use of small arms, ammunition, street and house fighting, and various forms of military drill. It was aimed specifically at Irish-American groups and ended with the exhortation:

Irishmen, swear by the sufferings of your millions starved to death by design, and buried without a coffin, swear by the blood and grief of your murdered and banished patriots, by the religion given to us by God himself, now degraded by your enemies, that you will in this great and glorious republic acquire the use of arms and study the art of war, and be ready for the day not far distant. Avengers—Fall in![9]

However impractical these military schemes in the long run, they preserved in the Irish underground the idea of military commitment.

Except for some wild and desperate plots of a terrorist nature hatched by Jeremiah O'Donovan Rossa who controlled a "skirmishing fund" gathered in the United States, the military designs of the Irish revolutionaries declined toward the end of the nineteenth century. It was not until the relentless John Devoy reorganized the secret society called the Clan-na-Gael (Children of the Gael) that the military dream became a practical operation again. In 1900 the Clan under Devoy circulated a bulletin to its members stating:

The object of the Clan is the complete independence of the Irish people and the establishment of an Irish Republic, and to unite all men of our race in all lands who believe in the principle that physical force is the only engine a revolutionary organization can consistently and successfully use to realize the hopes of lovers of freedom in lands subject to the bonds of oppression.[10]

As England moved into the tragedies of World War I, Devoy and the Clan-na-Gael plotted to get arms to Ireland. It was ironic that most of the nationalists in the South of Ireland began arming in imitation of the loyalist Orange North of Ireland groups who were ready to rebel against the Crown because of plans to grant Home Rule to Ireland.

The World War gave American agitators an opening to intrigue with Germany for arms for Ireland and to step up their support of the Irish underground in the old country. This was done, and the nationalists centered in Dublin requested funds for arms from America. This was the genesis of the armed guerrilla struggle that began with the Easter Rising in Dublin in 1916 and continued until 1921. During this entire period of ardent battle for Irish independence, the Irish organizations in America worked diligently to keep gun money and guns flowing to Ireland. The first patented Thompson submachine guns were smuggled from America to Ireland as the guerrilla war raged. The talents of men who had served with the American forces in France in World War I were brought into service. In terms of tactics, weaponry, and training, the Irish guerrilla war of independence was pretty much made on the spot, but it did receive some American arms. Above all, it received enormous encouragement and much direct financial aid from the Irish in the United States.[11]

The concourse of Irish nationalism and America was also an interplay of ideas and opinion. In the eighteenth and early nineteenth century there was a clear empathy between the two countries based upon their shared ideals and their mutual opposition to England. As American nativism arose, however, the flood of refugees from Ireland in the 1840s caused much alienation between the Irish and large blocs of Protestant Americans. This decline in general sympathy for Ireland was compensated for by the gradual growth of the Irish immigrant network in American political and social life after the American Civil War. When Charles Stewart Parnell launched his "Land War" in the 1880s it entailed a mighty effort to enlist American public opinion in behalf of land reform in Ireland. Parnell toured the United States addressing thronged meetings. People of all backgrounds gave to his cause. His sisters contacted Americans of social standing to form women's committees for his work. American newspapers and public figures were lavish in their praise of Parnell. This drive proved the value of American mass opinion for Irish nationalism.

During the years of Parliamentary maneuvering before World War I, moderate Irish-American opinion was carefully organized to benefit the Irish Parliamentary Party. Immigrant opinion was not neglected. Indeed, it was cultivated through numerous Irish-American newspapers, Catholic papers, and a continual series of lectures and events. Native American opinion was dealt with according to the skills of the Irish political leaders who had become strong powers in the urban areas of the country. Although their acquaintance with Irish conditions was often secondhand, and although they frequently put local allegiances first, on occasion they could be a potent force in behalf of Irish nationalist interests.

With the advent of the struggle for Irish independence a nationwide network of organizations and sympathetic opinion groups was available to help marshal general American opinion for the Irish cause. In a given major city there might be dozens of chapters of the Ancient Order of Hibernians, Irish county societies, the secret Clan-na-Gael, sympathetic labor unions composed of Irish members, political figures, Catholic school alumni groups, and literally hundreds of groups disposed to be of aid to Irish nationalism. These were mobilized between 1916 and 1921 to exert intense pressure on Congressmen, newspapers, government officials, and the American public at large. Millions of dollars were collected for the new Irish state. Although many bitter disputes raged among the leaders of the Irish communities about just how this help should be handled, it was largely handled effectively. Americans as a whole were led to sympathize with the Irish nationalist cause and to abhor the repressive policy of England in dealing with the Irish campaign for "self-determination."[12]

It is against this background of long-term Irish ties to America that the links between the Ulster violence of today and groups in the United States must be viewed. The provision of refuge, funds, military aid, and the leverage of sympathetic public opinion formed a tradition of partisanship for the underdog that accorded with native American sentiments. It also fitted into the American bloc voting pattern that gave many groups an influence in American opinion and policy far beyond their actual significance for American strategic interests. Armenians, Zionists, Poles, Cubans, and a wide variety of other groups have worked from America to realize nationalist aspirations.

The Irish-American connection to Irish nationalism was not by any means consistent. It took various forms and altered with both Irish and American changes of leadership and attitudes. It was spasmodic in its impact on Irish affairs, but it did have an impact that was far from negligible at critical junctures. It was not unusual to come across contemptuous references to the Irish-American connection in English sources, and these references, more often than not, reflected the class bias and hypocrisy that passed for social judgment among English commentators on Irish affairs. In Ireland, too, it was not unusual to encounter deprecating comments about the American enthusiasts for Irish nationalism. The cultural and political gap between Ireland and America was truly great, especially in the days when communications were poor. Misunderstandings easily arose. What linked the Irish nationalists and their American partisans, however, transcended the ordinary frictions and strains of a transoceanic alliance. It was the power of human sympathy, the power of an ancient enmity, and the mythic power of nationalist dedication with its heroism, defeats, resurrection, and promise of fulfillment. Despite all of the bombast and misconception this force prevailed and students of Irish nationalism knew it.

Since the establishment of an independent Irish state the American connection has not been dispensed with. The Treaty of 1921 setting up an Irish Free State was a compromise for those nationalists who desired a full Republic. These elements carried on a civil war from 1921 to 1923 tearing the fabric of Irish society in bitter conflict. Eventually the Republicans were driven underground or exiled. Many of them came to the United States where they intrigued to carry on the old fight against England, and also to subvert the political structure of the Free State. These diehards were often of socialist orientation. Many had been heroic partisans against the English and felt that the Treaty settlement allowing the setting up of a Protestant "statelet" in the Six Counties of Northern Ireland was a contradiction of all that Irish nationalism stood for. In the American cities they found organizations and resources to continue their agitation for a full thirty-two county Irish Republic that would embrace the entire island.[13]

In the 1930s riots between Protestants and Catholics in Belfast resulted in ferocious street fighting and widespread intimidation. The militant underground of the Irish Republican Army carried out a bombing campaign in England to bring home to the English public the fact that the Irish problem was far from settled by the Treaty of 1921. The bombing campaign just prior to World War II, designed to sabotage important facilities, is of some importance for an understanding of the future violent activities related to the Northern Ireland situation.

Joseph McGarrity, born in County Tyrone, made a fortune in Philadelphia and devoted his wealth and personal energies to Irish revolutionary work. He was a key figure in the mobilization of American resources in support of the Irish guerrilla war of the 1920s. Later he broke with Eamon de Valera and sided with the diehards who would not recognize de Valera's Irish state. McGarrity was a North of Ireland man, and it galled him that an English flag still flew over his childhood home. He was a rich and powerful man and head of the secret Clan-na-Gael. In the 1930s he maintained

contact with the IRA underground in Ireland. In 1938 when IRA leader
Sean Russell sought to launch a bombing campaign in England, the IRA
split. Old partisans like Tom Barry refused to back a campaign that would
bring civilian casualties. They felt the IRA was too weak to initiate a campaign in England.

McGarrity goaded Russell on, and the bombs began going off in England. Russell journeyed to Germany to try to work out joint plans with
that country as war with England approached. Both McGarrity and Russell
died soon thereafter, but their actions reached past their own lifetimes.
McGarrity was a believer in "the fanatic thing," the deed so dreadful that
men in positions in government would recognize the drastic resolution of
the revolutionary perpetrators of the deed.[14] Other IRA men like Tom
Barry did not share this view. Barry had a famous saying, "There are no
bad shots at ten yards range." His code, which was hard enough, put a
higher value on personal confrontation in guerrilla war than on terror
bombing. McGarrity's view extended the opening to terrorism that is always
present in guerrilla groups. From his base in America his relentless support
for armed action strongly perpetuated the old tradition of the American
connection to the revolutionary underground. His identity as a North of
Ireland man, too, confirmed the scheme of the IRA to make the issue of
the partition of Ireland the focus of their protracted war against the ves-
tiges of English colonialism on the island.

Ireland's neutrality during World War II, and the stiff criticism of that
country's neutral stand by such figures as Winston Churchill, eroded some
of the good will that Ireland had previously counted on in the United States.
Indeed, the United States Ambassador to Ireland during the war years
later wrote a vigorous pamphlet distributed by North of Ireland authorities
that extolled the partition of Ireland and decried attempts to end it. After
World War II Eamon de Valera, as head of the independent Irish government, decided to try to restore Ireland's international image. In the late
1940s his government launched a propaganda campaign against partition,
one feature of which was to make clear that it was the problem of partition
that had denied the Allies Irish cooperation in the war against Hitler. De
Valera visited the United States in 1949 and toured the country with his
message about the evils of the partition of Ireland. This kept the issue
prominent in the minds of Irish-Americans.[15]

It was in the 1950s that the resentment against the Protestant-dominated
North of Ireland government surfaced in deadlier form when the IRA carried out a series of raids across the border. These forays between 1954 and
1958 consisted of arms raids, shootings, bombing of border facilities, and
sabotage efforts. Once again the old symbolism of the "patriot game"
was activated. Martyrs such as the attractive and idealistic young Sean South,

one of the IRA men killed in the raids, were made. The image of the daring raiders going forth against hopeless odds was renewed. And again, the Protestant government and the government of the Twenty Six counties responded with a crackdown on known IRA leaders and internments.[16]

The IRA campaign of the 1950s was an admitted failure, except that it testified to the ability of the revolutionary underground to mend its shattered machinery and mount occasional offensives. De Valera in 1957 called again for discussions on the future of partition and proposed a Council of Ireland to blend the two portions of the island. The mounting prosperity of the 1950s somewhat diverted the attention of the Irish from what had become tired political slogans and issues that did not seem to gather any momentum. In the years after the IRA raids of the 1950s, the underground organization declined in adherents and in structure. Socialist influences in the cosmopolitan Dublin area began to receive more attention. For most of the Irish young people the tales of the twenties and the legacy of political disillusionment and contradictions of their parents' generation were easy to ignore. The world, even in conservative Ireland, was exciting and keyed to change. Ireland's future looked peaceful and prosperous.[17]

The prosperity of Ireland, so long delayed and so greatly relished, masked some grievous problems. Emigration continued; economic development was selective, often short-range and controlled from outside Ireland; social services were inadequate and many Irish institutions were unresponsive to the need for change. In Northern Ireland the contrast between progress and paralysis was especially acute. The old nineteenth-century industrial base had run down there as in the rest of the economy run from London. There had been much recruitment of new industry and this had been moderately successful but, like the "Operation Bootstrap" of the United States in Puerto Rico, it did not solve the underlying sickness and disparity of the area. The slums of Belfast and Derry were just as grim as ever. And most grotesquely the split between rich and poor, progress and impotence, the elect and the alienated, was largely along religious lines in the North of Ireland. Protestants ran the Six Counties through their one-party government, and Catholics scrabbled for what they could get in a religiously segregated society.[18]

Irish-American communities had changed a great deal since the watershed events of World War II. John Fitzgerald Kennedy had been elected President of the United States in a belated fulfillment of Irish-Catholic political aspirations. The social mobility and prosperity of America had further dispersed the Irish and dulled their consciousness of their own ethnic tradition. Their redoubts in the great cities where they had previously commanded powerful political machines had been eroded by the massive influx of blacks who were the new heirs to slums and to urban power.

The Vatican Council II had brought deeply unsettling changes to the Catholic Church that had been an emotional and institutional mainstay of Irish-Americans. A "youth culture" was turning young people away from the memories and affiliations of the past of their own families. The social and psychological bases of the long-established Irish-American tradition were shrinking. The old clubs, political organizations, business networks, and fraternities of feeling were breaking up.[19]

At the same time there were counter trends. Though not as powerful as the negative forces acting on the Irish-American tradition, they were still significant sources of vitality. Tourism was a major industry, and travel to Ireland was huge. Aer Lingus, Irish Airlines, was bringing £100,000,000 annually into Ireland by 1970 along with tens of thousands of American visitors. This not only kept the tourist image of Ireland alive with its compound of idyllic imagery and agreeable facilities, but it permitted a steady homecoming cycle for those who had emigrated to the United States. It also made it possible for some who were seriously interested in the future of Ireland to tour, study, and learn about Ireland. All of those young people who had been treated to literature courses in college in which Irish writings were extolled as "the greatest literature in the English language in the twentieth century," were now able to see the background firsthand. The tourist route was far different from the reality that had driven immigrants from Ireland by the droves, but it did tend to nourish the old Irish-American tie. For the emigrant, home for a visit, there was a different perception of the old country. They compared it to other places and other ways, and they were frequently critical.

For the thin ranks of old Irish rebels, the jet age seemed only to emphasize the perilous state of their hopes. In the Third World of former colonial nations all kinds of revolutionary groups were thriving. Algeria had forced France almost to revolution, and Africa and Asia were laced with revolutions. Fidel Castro even spurred a revolution ninety miles from the most powerful nation on earth. Where were the old ideals of the Irish Revolution? Was Ireland to go on forever with England's puppet state perched on the Six Counties? The old rebels asked. Nobody seemed to respond.

The peaceful exterior of Irish life was deceptive. Affluence had created its own brand of alienation and disgust at inequality. Change would come even to Northern Ireland, which was engaged in a hectic drive to import new industries. You could not have the new economy of abundance and forego its counterparts of social and political change. The new communications media such as television turned the local gaze outward daily, and it brought the inquiring world into the parochialism of Northern Ireland. That outside world was full of threatening currents: new revolutionary inspirations, a vastly increased arms market with all the weaponry of insurrection for sale, and success models of revolution scattered everywhere. The old rebels in their emaciated ranks would not have to wait long. Ireland's turbulent quest for full independence would re-emerge and with it the country's violent insurrectionary tradition. And when the old cause flashed in gunfire through the towns and villages of the North it would echo again in the United States—and the echo would be heard.

2

TERROR COMES

The coming of terror to Northern Ireland has received much mass media coverage, not only in Ireland and England, but in the United States. Most people have an emotional response to the killing and destruction, but the full chronology of the coming of terror is difficult to perceive. The pace of modern life tends to blur the true framework of events and leave only images and impressions. It is not necessary in the course of this examination to recite in detail the step-by-step advance of tragedy in Northern Ireland. But it is necessary as a prelude to understanding American connections to the violence, to have a general outline of the major phases of the deterioration of Ulster life since the late 1960s.

In 1963 it was clear to some people at least that change would come to the Protestant regime of the Six Counties. Captain Terence O'Neill, upper-class Protestant Premier of the Six Counties government, made tentative moves toward some new understanding with the Irish Republic and toward minimal internal reforms. Such moves gave the alarm to hard-liners like the Reverend Ian Paisley, an obscure pastor of a fundamentalist working-class Belfast congregation. Paisley and others raised the old cry of peril to Protestantism as any move was made to broaden Catholic participation in the life of the Six Counties.[1]

In 1967 members of the middle class, Catholics and others, formed the Northern Ireland Civil Rights Association to agitate for an expanded franchise for Catholics and for nondiscrimination in the allotment of publicly controlled housing in the towns throughout the North. The town of Dungannon was the center of this movement. Catholics there and elsewhere had long contended that voting districts were gerrymandered in favor of the ruling Protestant Unionist party and that housing discrimination was widespread.[2]

There has been much controversy as to the role that the IRA played with respect to the Civil Rights Association. The IRA, still dominated from Dublin, had espoused civil disobedience as a substitute for armed forays as a way of undermining the Six County government. It was ready to use protest marches, sit-ins, and the confrontation tactics of the civil rights movement as a vehicle for its own ends. Thus, one source of leadership for the Civil Rights Association was people with IRA background. Another was the student population of Queens University in Belfast, where young Catholics had begun to matriculate in greater numbers as a result of the slowly unfolding affluence of the 1960s. Socially conscious Catholics tended to favor the Northern Ireland Civil Rights Association and so did the small groups of Communists, Socialists, and radicals in the area.[3]

In October of 1968 a civil rights march in Derry, second largest of Northern Ireland's cities and a largely Catholic area, showed the growing strength of the movement. Premier Terence O'Neill stepped up his reform talk, and a Londonderry (the Protestant usage for the older name of Derry city) Commission was set up to supercede the Protestant-rigged local government in such key matters as housing allocation. Television coverage of the civil rights marches was increasing. The significance of this coverage was to be momentous. The 1960s had seen great waves of public emotional reaction aroused in the United States by television coverage of black civil rights marches and their often violent consequences. The citizen was brought face to face with the cruelty of racism in his own living room. Just as the fighting in Algeria was brought home to the French, and the dreadful scenes of Viet Nam would later be brought starkly onto the home screens of Americans, the television viewer's interest and emotions were aroused by the Northern Ireland civil rights activities. Irish and English viewers could feel the tension in the confrontations.

In January of 1969 a large group of members of the Civil Rights Association undertook a parade to Derry. The whole problem of marching parades had long been a legal and civic catspaw in Northern Ireland. Marches were banned and permitted with absurd inconsistency on the grounds of being threats to the public order. The march to Burntollet turned into a disaster when Protestants surrounded the Civil Rights Association ranks on a country road and battered the defenseless marchers with fury. The police escorts either would not or could not defend the marchers. This bloody demonstration became an emotional rallying point for even broader Catholic discontent in the North. What had begun as a campaign of middle-class do-gooders, some radicals, and students spread to become an extensive Catholic movement for reform of the Six County government.[4] Little Bernadette Devlin, a quick-tongued student with Socialist ideas, became one of the symbols of the movement, and on the strength of this was elected in April 1969 to the English Parliament as a member for Northern Ireland.

The month of August 1969 was a pivotal time for the fate of Northern Ireland. The summer parading of Civil Rights groups and the July 12 celebration of the traditional Protestant holiday marking the Battle of the Boyne victory of their forebearers in 1690 had made the scene tense. Clashes increased. In Derry a police riot sent uniformed members of the Royal Ulster Constabulary rampaging through the Catholic Bogside district. In Belfast the Catholic area along the Falls Road, long a scene of sectarian brutality, had been subjected to fierce Protestant assault. The situation in the North slipped toward anarchy. Rioting, intimidation, arson, sabotage of public facilities, and general mayhem broke loose. The police, largely Protestant, were unequal to it, as was the unreliable Protestant militia—the B-Special force—hated by the Catholics as a sectarian crowd of bully boys.[5]

In August, as disorder grew, England made a decision that was to haunt her. It was decided in London to send troops from England to preserve order. The problem was to be militarized. This was a fateful step. It may initially have diminished rioting and deterioration of order, but it also helped undermine the Northern Ireland government and placed the conflict on a new plane of antagonism. The presence of English armies in Ireland has ever been a stimulus to Irish nationalist endeavors, and this historic fact has apparently never been fully comprehended in England. The militarization of the conflict in Northern Ireland explains much of the tragedy that has ensued since 1969. Under the guise of humanitarian protection and defense of the rule of law, England sent an army to prop up a politically rotten regime. Her mistake was profound.

The eruption of violence in Belfast and Derry caught many by surprise. Numerous people in Northern Ireland had been heard to tell relatives and visitors prior to 1969 that the bad old days were gone, and that the gun would never come back into Irish politics. The summer of 1969 shocked them. The society of the Six Counties had lived with religious segregation, subtle discrimination, one party rule, and an official code of hypocrisy for fifty years, and it was hard for many to believe that it was not England, peaceful, settled, and devoted to the Queen.

In the working-class areas of the cities, however, life was not so insulated. Sectarian bitterness was never far below the surface, and sectarian frenzy always has been just a riot away. In these areas, when the storm of August 1969 hit, it prompted furious action. At first all was confused. When Protestant marauders assailed Catholic homes and businesses in Belfast, hasty "Citizens Defense Committees" formed vigilante groups to patrol and keep watch in the little streets. The IRA was hardly to be found. Having turned to civil disobedience in the 1950s, its previous military character had been eroded. Weapons were lacking and training had been neglected. The old IRA had become a frail network.

There had been a history of factionalism within the IRA, especially since it had changed from its militant stance. It was riven by conflicts of leadership, ideology, and regional viewpoints. The Belfast contingents of the organization shared this history. In 1964 the Belfast IRA had suffered a major factional split with the Dublin headquarters. William McKee, Seamus Toomy, Joe Cahill, and Sean McNelly had taken a position objecting to Dublin policies. At the root of the matter was the fact that the North of Ireland men thought self-defense should have a greater priority than the Dublin IRA's preoccupation with social goals and agitation. This seemingly tiny dispute was to have powerful consequences for Ireland after August 1969. Those men who had been jailed and harassed by the North of Ireland government for two generations now came out of the woodwork. By September 1969 the Provisional IRA had been formed in outline, and by December it had some 400 men in its ranks. They were arming as best they could. A few old Thompson submachine guns were still around, and handguns and hunting rifles were procured. The Catholic ghettoes of the North, which had first welcomed the British troops as defense against massacre, were now feeling the influence of the reconstructed IRA.[6]

The IRA was in an ambiguous position following the 1969 riots. It had been caught unaware. It had little armament. Its ranks were thin. The Catholic population was confused and fearful of a massive Protestant assault. In this confusion, despite reluctance born of better judgment, many did turn to the IRA as the only really helpful force in their besieged neighborhoods. As the British army became more and more active and as incidents of violence continued, the uneasy Catholic ghetto vigilantes turned to old IRA men for advice, weapons training, and some defense strategy in order to face an overwhelming British and Protestant threat.

As has been noted, the Northern Ireland violence was seen on news telecasts in the United States. Americans with relatives in the North and people who had visited there reacted emotionally to the spectacle. It seemed clear to many Irish-Americans in 1969 that the Protestant statelet that had ruled so unjustly for fifty years was unequal to the demands of democratic practice. The Catholic minority appeared clearly the underdog—surrounded and in peril. For those with families still in Derry and Belfast the peril was palpable. Relatives in Derry or Belfast were actually telephoning New York and Philadelphia in tears and fright, begging for guns and aid, terrified that the next night would bring massacre at the hands of the Orange mobs and police. This was one kind of stimulus to Irish-American engagement with the problem, and it was a galvanizing one for those who emigrated from Ulster and knew the depths of local hatred.

In the midst of the publicity waves that raised again the old stereotype of a miserable Ireland, land of strife and battle, civil rights activist Bernadette Devlin flew to the United States. On August 22 she announced that she would tour the United States to raise funds in seven figures for the Northern Ireland Civil Rights Association. Her trip was well publicized, and she was something of a media darling. Although not beautiful, she had a true spark of sharp, fresh intelligence, a rare enough commodity on United States television. Her responses to interviewers were tart and quotable. She made no bones about her Marxism, her sympathy with black civil rights aspirations in the United States, and her contempt for the Irish bourgeoisie. This compound of views created no little consternation among the essentially conservative Irish Catholics who were Miss Devlin's prime audience. These views, added to the youth of the fiery activist, cast a pall over her tour. Somewhere in the heartland of the United States, she gave up in disgust and returned home.

Irish-Americans were not prepared for the radicalism brewed in the cauldron of the North of Ireland. They could appreciate a straight old-line Protestant-Catholic struggle—at least the more religiously oriented could— but the complexity of social issues presented by Bernadette Devlin was a bit beyond them.[7] Irish Catholics had a sorry record of antagonism toward blacks dating from the days of dogfighting in the inner-city ghettoes of America. Ties between the United States blacks and their needs and those of the Ulster minority were beyond their grasp. However, Bernadette Devlin did raise some $200,000 for the Northern Ireland Civil Rights Association. Her trip brought out the "ancients" who remembered the 1920s and the crusade for Irish independence. The old ones, ironically, understood little Bernadette, although they might not agree with her social views. When it came to struggle, the code of the old Clan-na-Gael members said, "Don't be too choosy about who you take help from."

The events of 1969 set in motion the Northern Ireland dynamics of destruction. England clamped an armed intervention on the Six Counties. The IRA was revived on an ad hoc basis in a purely local response to Protestant onslaught. But the IRA came from an old and hard school. The lessons of the past were unearthed for restudy. The underground reached out to the Irish Republic to the south, to England and to America. Old lines of communication and intrigue were rejuvenated. Locally, the Provisional IRA built up its leadership. There were sharp differences with the Dublin Official IRA, but the men in Ulster were on the spot and knew their situation, and as their activity increased, they outnumbered and upstaged their Official counterparts. The split between locally-oriented Provisionals and Marxist-oriented officials led to several armed clashes, and this helped to seal the estrangement.

In May 1970 the Irish Republic was shaken by a cabinet scandal that led to the ousting of cabinet members Neil Blaney, Charles Haughey, and Kevin Boland. They were allegedly involved in a gunrunning plot to aid

Catholics in the North. This was just the kind of cross-border skulduggery that made Northern Protestants froth with rage, and the government of Irish leader Jack Lynch was under intense pressure from London not to let such things occur.[8] Adopting the title and role of peacemaker, England set herself up as arbiter of the Ulster struggle, and she did not want the Irish Republic to further roil the waters. Strong blocs of opinion in the Republic, however, bitterly resented English arms in the North and believed the Republic had as least as much right to send weapons into the Six Counties as England had. Considering the state of opinion with which the Irish Republic's leader Jack Lynch had to deal, his government had acted with considerable circumspection. A stronger and more tightly organized government would have been much more direct in aiding beleaguered compatriots so near at hand. For example both Greeks and Turks displayed a more active and direct partisanship in the disorders on Cyprus.

It was in mid-1970 that the specter of chaos really began to stalk the streets of Northern Ireland. In July 1970 the British army carried out brutal raids in Catholic areas in Belfast, ignoring Protestant areas where there was equal cause to suspect arms stockpiling. By autumn the IRA had built strength and was carrying out selected violence, organizing riots and sniping incidents. In 1971 the Provisional IRA, still at odds with the Marxist Official branch, faced large scale recruiting growth by the Ulster Defense Regiment, a potent opposition of Protestants.

Few people in Northern Ireland will forget the summer of 1971. In July there were mass roundups of suspected IRA men carried out with summary illegality. The date of most signal uproar, however, was August 9 when mass internment without charge or even cause was instituted. This was a desperate Unionist measure. It caused a horrendous outpouring of Catholic resentment. It was a draconian action not seen since the Nazis had rounded up Jews and others during their frenzy of war and destruction. Men were pulled from their beds and dragged to trucks, carted away, tortured and thrown into prison without any semblance of legal due process or even identifiable accusations against them. Refugees poured out of the North into the Irish Republic. There were thirty deaths in riots. Northern Ireland was closer to civil war in August 1971 than at any time in fifty years. As the roar subsided somewhat the stock English military assertion that the IRA was "virtually beaten" was once again bruited forth for the consumption of the media.

Following internment and weeks of riot and intimidation across religious lines, it is estimated that nine thousand people left Belfast. Britain was shocked by the dimensions of the fury. Foreign Secretary Reginald Maudling even confessed that perhaps the subject of some Catholic participation in the Northern Ireland government might be discussed. Representatives of the Irish Republic, England, and the Northern Ireland government came together for talks. The year 1971 closed after Dutch officials confiscated a shipment of arms intended for the IRA at Schipol airport. Spokesmen for the Provisional IRA stated that their organization was indeed short of arms, but they also announced a program that has remained largely unchanged through several years of guerrilla fighting. Its goals were:

An end to English army occupation of Ulster.
Abolition of the Stormont government.
A regional parliament freely elected with minority participation.
Release of all political prisoners.
Compensation for all who suffered under English violence.[9]

If internment without charge and its attendant disorders was the emotional high point of 1971, the Derry massacre on January 30, 1972 was probably the most somber and anger-wracked crisis of 1972. A march of Catholics in Derry was fired upon by English paratroops. Thirteen people were killed. Rioters in the Irish Republic burned the British Embassy in Dublin. World opinion was aghast that the English army could have blundered so shamefully and so stupidly in the midst of such a tense community situation. A retaliation bombing in Aldershot, England took seven lives. The tragedy of the Derry slayings was heightened when Lord Widgery later issued a report whitewashing the incident.[10]

These events of 1971 and 1972 were like an emotional hurricane for the Irish in Ulster—and for many elsewhere as well. Bombing, shooting, and rampant repression created mad scenes for television photographers' cameras day after day. The arrogant and crippled Stormont government finally outlived its usefulness at the end of March 1972, and London declared it suspended with the same patronizing power that had been used to concoct and uphold it. Direct rule of Northern Ireland from London was imposed. In the spring a women's peace movement developed in Belfast as the population continued to suffer all manner of abuse and disruption due to the continuing violence. The Provisional IRA reaffirmed its own peace terms: England and her army must get out; amnesty for political prisoners must be granted; and a representative government formed.

The sequence, manic fury, and brutal significance of all these happenings worked like a relentless storm upon Irish opinion in the North. A three cornered struggle reeled everywhere, with the English sometimes fighting the IRA and sometimes Protestant rioters and vigilantes. Whereas Mr. Justice Scammon had issued a report in April 1972 saying that the original disorders were not part of any insurrection plot in 1968 and 1969, the Catholic population had been driven close to insurrection by such events as internment and the Derry slayings. The Provisional IRA, its support ebbing and flowing with the tide of army repression and public outrage, was, of course, now committed to insurrection and beyond. It sought to make Northern Ireland ungovernable and to drive some bloody bargain with the Protestant population.

In three short years England had succeeded, in company with the Northern Ireland government, in squandering all of the good will that had been built up with Ireland as a whole over two generations. She had, in addition, opened again that ancient and inglorious wound of relations with Ireland that had cost her so much. London was paying a horrible price for defending her foothold in Ireland.

In the United States in 1968-69 groups had formed calling themselves the Friends of the Northern Ireland Civil Rights Association. They were composed of immigrants from Northern Ireland, other Irish people, and liberal Americans of many backgrounds. In December 1971 in a large advertisement in the *New York Times* it was announced that The American Committee for Ulster Justice had been formed with a number of notables listed as members. This committee was to embrace people of any religious persuasion willing to work for justice and peace in Northern Ireland. It was composed, however, of persons almost entirely from New York. As the pace of events became more hectic, an organization called Irish Northern Aid became increasingly active in collecting funds for relief in Northern Ireland. These groups were the nucleus of the organized effort in the United States to bring American opinion and assistance to bear on the Northern Ireland problem.[11]

While the reaction of Americans with strong Irish ties was aroused by the escalating violence in Ulster, Protestants of many denominations resented the picture of Protestant tyranny that had been the initial newscaster's portrait of government in the North. They resented, too, the terrible violence that had been visited on Protestant Irishmen by the crisis. Irish Catholics, not unexpectedly, took an opposite course in their sympathies. Whatever their backgrounds, however, Americans were given as full a treatment of the situation as the format of their news media would permit. News reports, television specials, *Time* magazine cover stories, and almost daily newspaper coverage catalogued the crisis.

The mass media coverage of the events in Northern Ireland was crucial for subsequent developments. As with the events of the United States civil rights struggle in the 1960s and the coverage of the Viet Nam war, the confrontation of the American public with violence had a deeply disturbing effect. The riots and bombings in Ulster spoke for themselves. Here was a society in desperate struggle. The background of the struggle, although summarized rather effectively by numerous magazines and newspapers, left most Americans perplexed. After all, what seemed a religious war of seventeenth century origins and ferocity was not exactly a comprehensible thing to Americans living in a secular society.

An initial impulse of the activists for the minority in Northern Ireland was to seek to tell their story to the American public generally. There is still harbored abroad that nostalgic notion that America is the special friend of oppressed minorities, so it was natural that the Catholic leaders would seek to appeal to American opinion. The specific purpose of this appeal was far from clear, but Bernadette Devlin and Ulster minority leaders Gerry Fitt and John Hume duly gave interviews and appeared on telecasts. Protestant leaders, in turn, complained bitterly that the American press was biased in favor of the Catholics and was giving publicity to political incendiaries and social renegades.

In addition to the theme of violence, the mass media, then, had the arguments of the respective antagonists to deal with. Because of the articulate flair of the Catholic leaders and the daring background of the IRA so long portrayed on stage and screen, the Catholics did seem to have the edge. The mass media, and television in particular, thrive upon dramatization of the personalities and Bernadette Devlin with her caustic, impish flaggellations of the one-party Protestant regime of the North was fascinating camera fare. Less intelligible to the American audience, but still a bizarre figure, was the Rev. Ian Paisley, defender of the faith of hard rock Protestantism. This minister of a Belfast working class congregation had attended Bob Jones University in the United States, a fundamentalist school with strict religious training. Rev. Paisley was a Bible bombast of the old school, a hellfire-and-damnation-prophet predicting doom and Roman Catholic Armageddon if Ulster Protestants did not stand fast against civil rights, outside pressure, and the IRA. Rev. Paisley was good copy when set against Bernadette Devlin. He visited the United States in the summer of 1969 and had as one of his hosts the Rev. Carl McIntyre, another fundamentalist leader whose particular phobia was Communism. Rev. Paisley's trip did not match that of Bernadette Devlin in propaganda effect, but it did serve to give a sense of the intractability of the two sides in Northern Ireland.

In the wake of these two media "stars" there came a steady trickle of other speakers from Northern Ireland. These were men not so well known. They did not get much television coverage. They appeared in the little halls of the Irish clubs in the major cities. Their message was potent. It was a firsthand battle report from relatives and besieged residents in Belfast and Derry. It was delivered with raw Irish emotional effectiveness. It followed up the generalized media coverage with specifics. It told Irish Americans in these sessions that their old primary school had been raided and the children roughly searched, that the old parish church had been burned, that such and such a relative was on the run, or in Long Kesh prison camp

without charge, or released from prison after being tortured. People wept
openly at these sessions and the gatherings breathed rage at every sentence.
Added to the general news coverage, these gatherings were surging stimu-
lants to the Irish who heard them.

The torture revelations from Northern Ireland were especially harrowing,
and they had their searing impact on IRA sympathizers. Amnesty International in London revealed that both random brutality on the part of
troops, and carefully calculated and sophisticated torture methods devised
for use in counter-insurgency operations were freely used in the North.[12]
In February 1972 the British Society for Social Responsibility in Science
criticized a report prepared for the British government by Sir Edmund
Compton denying torture allegations. The scientists declared the methods
of psychological disorientation used by the army interrogators in Northern
Ireland to be directly derived from methods used by the Russian KGB.
Doctors in the Irish Republic examined released internees from the North
and found dreadful damage to both mind and body. In 1972 Dr. Rona
Fields of the University of Southern California wrote that her studies of
those alleging torture in the North showed that psychological and physical
torture had been practiced upon internees as a matter of course. That such
vicious tactics had been used by English authorities while they posed as
peaceful referees holding apart two raving Irish factions simply heightened
the disgusted reactions of decent people and of Irish-Americans in particular.

The Irish-Americans were not slow to point out the deprivation of
human rights involved in the Northern Ireland repression. The representatives of the Irish Republic argued conclusively before the human rights
tribunal of the European Human Rights Commission that there had been
widespread and systematic violations. In the United States these arguments
were presented by those working in behalf of the Catholic minority in
the North of Ireland. The American public had, however, been surfeited
with such cries of anguish. It could react to televised violence, but not
legal documentation. The civil rights campaigns of blacks, the ravages of
human dignity in Viet Nam, the imprisonments of Soviet Jews had all
been widely publicized. The Irish allegations were lost in the welter of noise
distracting American listeners. The events of the 1960s had largely blunted
the American pretense to a special concern in international law for those
who suffered everywhere. To some, however, it still mattered.

Thus, general news coverage, the appearance of special personalities,
the vividness of the portrayal of violence by Irish speakers touring the
United States, the revelations of torture of internees, and the seeming isolation of the Irish struggle from world opinion all had the effect of deeply
arousing Americans who had special ties to the North. They were profoundly
disturbed by the events since 1969. The coming of terror placed them in a

39564

position of intense frustration. If they had been in Ireland, they could have reacted in some concrete way to the situation according to their individual dispositions. In the United States all they could do was to fume at first, or make a hurried visit home to Armagh or Coleraine to see the troops, the armored cars, and to confirm for themselves the brutal reality of it all. The crisis in Northern Ireland conditioned Irish people in the United States to hunt for a response that they could make, to find some way in which they could do something about the conflict there.

While Irish-American opinion was in the throes of indecision, the IRA in Ulster had reaffirmed its link with the old tradition of guerilla action, and moved to absorb the lessons of all those groups from Indochina to Israel to Cuba who had waged underground war. Some of the IRA men had been in English prisons in the 1960s with the followers of General Grivas who had fought the Turks in Cyprus. English officials in Cyprus had snared these men in another of those international imbroglios that always seem to involve English troops far, far away from England. There had been exchanges of information between Irishmen and Greek Cypriot. Men in the same profession do tend to gravitate together, and those committed to underground war are no exception, so the IRA had no great difficulty in opening up sources of information and technical aid.

The IRA experience in the border campaign of the 1950s was really a rerun of tactics used in the 1920s with some improved firing power. The development of modern underground war, however, had made explicit several precepts that required new IRA attention. First, the new warfare was more secret, more urban, and had more general targets than the Irish struggle of the 1920s. The vigilant Protestants of the North and the more highly developed English intelligence cadres posed problems, if not essentially different, at least of a new dimension for the IRA. There was a Sunday in 1920 when the men of Michael Collins's death squads wiped out British intelligence in one fierce coordinated campaign in Dublin. Times were a bit different now. The goal of the guerrillas in the 1970s was not only to harrass and tie down troops by inflicting damage on them, and to make Northern Ireland ungovernable but to cement the Catholics behind the IRA. These goals had many contradictions hidden within them. To bring society to a grinding halt would penalize Catholics as well as Protestants. To kill troops meant killing civilians too on occasion. It was a different kind of warfare from the days of old Tom Barry's flying column roving the misty Irish countryside.

There had been considerable strife in the Ireland of the 1920s in the cities of Dublin, Belfast, and other centers. The IRA knew the alleys and plenty of back street tactics. A modern technological city like Belfast, however, had built up much stronger networks of communications than existed in the 1920s. It was more complex. It required more careful analysis by those who would subject it to misery. The guerrillas in other places, the FLN in Algiers, the OAS in France, had sidestepped this issue of the complexity of the urban environment. They had simply resorted to terror to create urban panic. Selective targeting was carried out on the basis of what would produce terror in the urban crowds. The IRA accepted this precept, and this was a great departure, at least in terms of the legend of the organization. The old IRA had indeed carried out bombing campaigns, most notably those in England. The IRA had never had to resort to terrorizing large numbers of the Irish people. Cooperation had been there, as had opposition, but mass cowing of the people with sheer terror had been a tactic pursued by the hated Black and Tan auxiliaries under a classically stupid English policy of the 1920s. The acceptance of the terror tactics of the modern guerrilla undergrounds was to take a terrible toll in civilian casualties in Northern Ireland, and it was to deprive the IRA of much more widespread support in the United States. IRA spokesmen have said that the bombing was not an imported tactic, and that it was simply aimed at wrecking business in cities and towns, and putting the business class under pressure. Perhaps a lack of arms led to bombing campaigns that blasted bus stations, department stores, and pubs, but the indiscriminate nature of the planted bomb as a weapon fearfully compromised the Provisional IRA in both Irish and American opinion.

If the nature of modern guerrilla warfare in a mixed population of enemies and sympathizers brought new problems, and if the use of terror bombing created difficulties of a new magnitude, a third characteristic of the new underground war also changed older assumptions. Guerrillas need support. They are not self-contained army groups, but more often are part-time networks that emerge and fade into the general population. Sanctuaries of the most ingenious kind are needed to hide and cover the partisans. Chairman Mao's analogy of the guerrilla as a fish in the fluid of the mass population was not too applicable in Ulster. The Provisional IRA had sanctuaries in the North when Catholic areas there were cordoned off as "no go" districts by the British army. When English authority was reasserted over these areas in 1970 and 1971, their use as sanctuaries became most difficult. The areas across the border in the Irish Republic were also sanctuaries, but when English pressure forced the Irish government to increase border security, these became more difficult to use. The United States and England were, because of distance, of limited use as sanctuaries, although they could be used for arms smuggling, financial support, and refuge on a long-term basis. The problem of sanctuary in Northern Ireland led expediently to IRA intimidation of Catholics in order to find hide-outs, communication posts, and other operational links.[13]

The use of terror bombing, the retaliations visited on Catholics for IRA activities, the intimidation to gain room to operate all placed strains on the Northern minority. If English torture of captives was horrible, so was the bombing of a crowded Belfast restaurant full of women and children, and the Irish in the United States had to weigh these horrors to keep their commitment to the guerrilla war. The sympathizers with the Provisional IRA did this. In their minds and emotions they weighed the horrors, and they kept their allegiance to the Provos. Stories about the IRA buying the services of pre-adolescents as "teeny bombers" circulated as imprisonments and casualties cut the number of available IRA men in 1972 and 1973. The use of women as IRA auxiliaries did not bother the Irish for the Irish tradition is replete with numerous heroines who fought beside their men. The psychology of antagonism against the English and their Northern Unionist allies was so deep that these morbid practices did not sway the allegiance of the tight network of believers needed for an American-based support network. The mentality of anti-English traditionalism was so steeped in the vast catalog of English injustice in Ireland that the end of opposing that English force and guile was judged to justify practically any means.

It is appropriate to look beyond nationalism as an ideology in seeking an explanation for Irish recourse to violence. As with many oppressed peoples there is still a stigma attached to the Irish, an attribution of inferiority that carries with it a special imputation of habitual violence. It is commonly expressed in the disdainful English expostulation that generally runs, "Oh, the Irish, at it again, fighting and killing one another." Such comments are traditional clichés among the English who have had such a horrific record of warring on people in underdeveloped areas, and who are constantly surprised by the counterviolence. This kind of cliché-judgment about the Irish is not uncommon in the United States as well. Such a stereotyped view, derived from the history of strife in Ireland and outbursts of violence that accompanied immigrant struggles in America, is a crude enough observation, but its worst feature is that it implies a special and inherited—and somehow inevitable—quality of violence among those described by it.

Ireland, like most nations, has a long history of both peace and violence. While Ireland was renowned for wars of internal conquest, it was also renowned for extraordinary monastic traditions reaching back to the fifth century. The peaceful missionaries from Ireland in early medieval times helped pacify barbarian Europe. Because of the violent portion of its history, however, Ireland and the Irish are seen as especially prone to agitation, fighting, and war. Analysis of such generalized perception reveals that in actuality the Irish have been simply vulnerable humans, responding largely in the same way that others do to the forces acting on them. The forces acting on them may be more disruptive and the cultural context more distressed because of the nature of Irish history. The country was an island fought over by waves of foreigners.

Modern social analysis makes clear that the sources of violence are diverse. There may be genetic or hormonal differences among people that make some more passionate or aggressive than others, but Ireland's genetic heritage is so diverse due to repeated invasions and mingling of peoples that there can hardly be any argument for a collective genetic predisposition toward violence. If there is an innate aggression in people, there is no reason to believe the Irish have more of it than their neighbors the English, who circled the globe for several centuries conquering other peoples. If violence arises from frustration, then Ireland deserves credit for evincing more than most places, for the poverty and lack of fulfillment in its life would indeed promote frustration. If insecurity is posited as the cause of violence, then the marginal employment and social status of both Catholics and Protestants in Ulster could be credited with prompting a neurotic lashing out by the victims. Alienation from the prevailing order is another hypothesis to explain violence. The prolonged alienation of Ulster Catholics, their lack of hope for change, seems to fit this theory. The breakdown of social systems is said to generate violence, and the decay of Stormont's rule in Northern Ireland and the challenges to its claims of ascendency could be part of the motive force for the area's violence. Perhaps one of the key explanations of the turmoil there is the defective socialization of each new generation, subject to the local religious divisions. The old-fashioned religious ideas of the area make both Protestants and Catholics suspicious of sensual pleasure, yet psychologists believe that rewards of bodily pleasure are important to the early assurance of a stable personality and to the pacification of the spirit. There is not much room for such pacification even of infants in the slums of Derry or Belfast.

Whatever the root causes of Irish violence, they are explicable in terms of local social conditions and intervening influences that shape local life. These causes also have effects that become a part of the personality of those who emigrate from Ireland. This is one reason there is a following in the United States for the guerrillas and why there is an American-Irish underground.

3

NETWORK FOR THE NORTH

America is so vast, diverse, and active that many kinds of things can transpire almost without notice. For generations, Mexicans and Cubans, Chinese and Irishmen have conspired in America to work for political changes in their homelands, and most Americans have been blissfully ignorant of their activities except during some transient crisis or public furor. Although such exile political groups seek publicity, their campaigns are usually tiny compared with the roar of regular news coverage that thunders through America daily. So it has been with the Irish who are partisans of their kinfolk in the North of Ireland. Their organized activity proceeds relatively unheeded amid the clangor and blare of American life. Yet, it is a persistent activity. It is small in scale, but significant in relation to the problem of Ulster. It has, as has been indicated, the weight of a long and fiery tradition behind it. It accords with the American tradition that ambiguously favors minorities, underdogs, and immigrants seeking refuge from oppression in other lands.

Since 1969 there has grown up in the United States a network of Irish aid for the Catholic minority in the North of Ireland. Its components bear study not only as elements of Irish overseas political agitation, but as part of the international web of revolutionary support groups that function in behalf of many causes and countries. The network invites study, too, because of its position in the American spectrum of subcultural group life. Just how such a web functions in contemporary America is of interest, for even smaller groups have had great impact. The mind moves back to Sarajevo and a tiny circle of Serbian youths.

The backbone of the IRA support groups in the United States is composed of people with North of Ireland ties. The ties are often of blood, and hardly anything could be stronger in the Irish context. Families in Ireland have maintained ties despite fantastic histories of emigration. Young people go away to Australia or South Africa. They emigrate to California or Canada. They migrate habitually to England to work. Yet the families maintain contact. They write, visit, and remember one another. It is all linked to the psychology and emotional memories of childhood. People raised in the warmth and ambient beauty of the Irish communities scattered through a lovely landscape cannot escape the memory. It is a lovely recollection of childtime. Though a boy may have been raised in the bitterness of Derry slums, he knows that only a short walk away is the deep beauty of hills and mountains of his native area, the beauty of timeless Erin, breathing legend across the landscape.

For the Irish overseas, there is also the recollection of that long struggle of Irish patriotism and melancholy sacrifice. There is the direct tie to people living in the contemporary struggle in Northern Ireland. There is your sister back there, shopping with English guns pointed at her, sending her children to school through barricades guarded by English troops. There is your kind old aunt whose house was torn apart by searching paratroops. There is the cemetery where your grandparents are buried, now the site of an English machine gun emplacement. Such things tear at people who know that their nation has been smashed repeatedly by the power still represented in that English Army. To look at modern Ireland, to see its weakness, its scars of exploitation, the demographic and social vulnerability of the island, and to know that England worked the greater part of this, does things to the minds of Irishmen.

Rosemary Harris in her book, *Prejudice and Tolerance in Ulster,* reveals something about Northern Ireland families. The picture is one of tightly knit people, committed by birth to the codes of their religious groups with the enormous fund of precedent and allegiance that this implies. They are prejudiced in that they believe the stereotypes that alienate them from those of the other religion. They prejudge Catholics and Protestants and this sets the expectations and practices by which they live. It is not just the Protestants who are prejudiced, but the minority Catholics as well, though perhaps to a less morbid extent. The respective religious communities in Northern Ireland actually intensify their own group life by the exclusion and circumvention that their religious separatism enjoins upon them. Thus, the Catholics who emigrate to the United States from the area come from an especially intense group culture. Their loyalty has been tested even in childhood. They do not lose their group affiliation or thought patterns simply by emigrating to America. Indeed, distance from the homeland may even make them more sensitive, more emotionally committed to the values of their group, or at least to selected portions of those values.[1]

On coming to America the old methods of mutual aid still hold among the immigrants. It is rare when an Irishman will turn up at some Nationalities Service Center or other immigrant aid organization. Family and friends provide guidance and aid. Jobs are gotten, lodgings found, football clubs joined, and all the organization required is drawn from the Irish kinship and friendship circle. This reinforces the sense of identity overseas.

In addition to those with living relatives in the tension of Northern Ireland, there are Irish people from other areas who are supporters of the Northern minority viewpoint. They may simply be people with their own family traditions of Irish nationalism, or they may be people with strong responses to all the news of violence and suffering in the North. Some of these, for instance, may be members of Clan-na-Gael clubs, or Irish Republican Clubs, or some other organizations committed to eradication of British rule in the North. It is difficult to encounter Irish-born people who, though not North of Ireland in birth, do not react strongly to English presence in Ulster. Often people not born in Ulster react to the social pressure of those who were.

There is a constant complaint among English government leaders, echoed by the Dublin elite as well, that those in the United States contributing toward the violence in the North are a collection of addled, sentimental, duped Irish-Americans of the St. Patrick's Day parade variety.[2] This thought may be reassuring to those who utter it, but it is simply untrue. The people supporting the activist network in the United States are hard-bitten North of Ireland types, whether actually born there or not. They are not zany bog men or fatuous American blarney stone lovers. They are mostly people with direct experience with the North, steeped in its rancor, and gritty as the stones of Antrim. They do not shrink from dreadful acts. "We will never give up!" is their motto. If activists are American-born they tend to be people who have generally come through a hard school themselves, who perhaps served in one or more of America's brutalizing wars, and are imbued with a high tolerance for violence, a tolerance that has become something of a characteristic of Americans. The IRA support network is not an Aer Lingus tourist crowd. It is more like an overseas extension of the Falls Road ghetto.

If Ulster-born people are the backbone of the network that supports IRA activity in Northern Ireland, and if they are abetted by other Irish-born people and native Irish-Americans, there are ancillary chains of sympathy and assistance that are woven into the network. Journalists are allies, not because they share uncritically the full nationalist view of the North of Ireland problem, but simply because they cover the news and tell the story of the conflict. Some writers like Pete Hamill of the *Village Voice* in New York and Jimmy Breslin are strongly sympathetic to the Catholic minority in their writings.[3] Others are partisan only intermittently. Still, they tell the story, and as journalists this simple fact makes them subject to the influences of those who have a story to relate and who want the story told in a certain way.

Another skein of influence extends to and through the fraternity of civil libertarians in the United States whose concern it is to seek an impartial rule of law and defense of human rights in all societies. The beginning of the North of Ireland struggle in 1969 was a civil rights campaign asking only those legal protections consonant with general democratic practice among Western nations. The attention and sympathy of partisans of civil liberty focused on Ulster when international publicity thrust long neglected conditions there into sensational limelight. Civil libertarians in the United States were especially interested, not only in view of the historic ties to Ireland, but also because there was a heightened perception of civil rights issues in the 1960s. Black protests, marches, and campaigns had made the nation aware of the terminology of civil rights. A far from negligible factor for the kind of literate people likely to be attentive to civil rights was the fact that the story of Irish rebellion, aspiration, and political trauma had been cast in great drama and literature in this century. Altogether, the civil rights theme was an especially important one through which Americans could interpret the North of Ireland issue.[4]

In the big cities, where the old-style machine politics still partially held sway, the Democratic party's legacy of Irish leadership disposed some politicians to advert to the Northern Ireland issue. Senator Ted Kennedy, Senator Abraham Ribicoff, and others addressed the issue in terms of international responsibility. Members of the House of Representatives phrased resolutions and issued some press releases. There was some resolution-lofting in some state legislatures, and local politicians duly declared for brotherhood and Irish freedom. These political elements had some vested interest, as well as some true personal emotional sentiments, bound up with the Irish problem. They had access to the media, and they did the natural thing in delivering opinions on a topic that was of interest to numbers of their constituents.[5] The outraged cries of distress from London about such statements were also quite natural considering British pretensions to pristine purity of policy in Ulster.

There had grown up in the 1960s a youth culture and a keenly restive radicalism in many countries that exercised itself in protests, marches, and indulgence in a critical counterculture. This youthful radicalism, at times mere juvenile posturing, at times seriously revolutionary, had its antecedents in American populist history. It was flagrant enough in style to horrify that American Gothic conscience enshrined in "middle America." The Weathermen, the Students for a Democratic Society, the Socialist Workers Party readily sympathized with the Irish underdogs who opposed a Unionist regime in Northern Ireland encrusted with the hoary accolades of Tory capitalism. The sympathy of American radicals gave the Irish dissidents allies on campuses, in the radical press, and among theoreticians and avid young revolutionaries.

There were also specialized groups of humanitarians concerned with the Irish problem. Amnesty International played a laudable role in exposing the torture and prison brutality practiced with repulsive hypocrisy by the English army and overlords in Ulster. The Quakers helped organize prison visits for relatives of those who had been so miscellaneously interned by the English.[6] Many American organizations, such as the National Conference of Christians and Jews, however, maintained a quite uncharacteristic silence about the North of Ireland problem and its implications for Americans. This silence contrasted with the very active campaigns in behalf of Soviet Jews, for instance, and the contrast was not unobserved by acid Irish commentators. The distortions and myopia of American liberal opinion did not go without Irish comment, and the inconsistency was picked up by radical critics as well.

Beyond these groups there was that huge continental babble known as general American opinion, the distracted and querulous nature of which it was the task of TV commentators to divine. The Viet Nam War, the abrasions of race relations, the striving for nostalgic repose and the whirligig of changing mores made this opinion fretful and deeply uneasy. It reacted to world crises and international disruptions, Irish or otherwise, with an irritation bordering on exhaustion. Only the young had the energy to grieve seriously over these problems, it seemed.

In the 1920s when the Irish mobilized in the United States to aid the fight of the old country for independence, they could rely on certain time-honored resources. The Irish-born population and those with Irish parents numbered over four million. Millions of others were much closer in attachment to Ireland than they would be in the 1970s. The major cities were honeycombed with Irish groups, and the Catholic church was a medium of sympathy and communication that was eventually to become responsive to facilitating work for Irish freedom. In the America of the 1920s life was not so complex and Irish political power was still tremendous. There was, too, the fact that all of Ireland was involved in that struggle, and the issues were seemingly clear-cut to the Irish-American mentality, even though there was considerable factionalism.

In 1970 America's Irish-born population was only 290,000.[7] The Irish organizations were a mere shadow of former strength. The Catholic church in the age of ecumenicism was loathe to open old Protestant-Catholic vendettas, and besides, it was having its own fill of disruption with hippie priests, antiwar activists, strident nuns, and a crisis of institutional confidence. Irish political power in the cities, though still significant, was not a mainstream force for the determination of foreign or public policy.[8] And, the Northern Ireland troubles simply did not engage all Irish-born or Irish-American people. Many believed that Ireland's major problems were rooted in economic, social, and religious conditions largely independent of England and Northern Ireland.

Thus, the activists sympathetic to the Provisional IRA had their work cut out for them. They had to begin with what resources they had, and these rarely included prominent Americans of Irish extraction. Such people in their self-conscious success avoided controversies not germane to their immediate interests, and would certainly avoid controversies involving mass bombings in Ireland. Ironically, they might approve United States terror bombing in Viet Nam, but Northern Ireland was another story.

The activists clustered around the major center of Irish Northern Aid operations at 273 E. 194th Street in New York City knew that there was still a small network of Irish organizations in each of the major American cities. County societies, the Ancient Order of Hibernians, beneficial societies, tiny Irish Republican circles, the remnants of the Clan-na-Gael, and other organizations held their meetings, kept their halls rented, and drew Irish people to annual rounds of events. *The Irish World,* once Patrick Ford's powerful New York weekly, was now 100 years old, much reduced and bland. *The Irish Echo,* edited for years by a spectacularly fiery character named Charles Connolly, was now temperate and small in circulation. The few other Irish papers were negligible. In some cities there were Irish radio programs of news and folk music. Beyond this rather emaciated framework there was little that could be counted on. Even within it there was estrangement, confusion of viewpoints, and a general perplexity about what could be done in any practical way about the Northern Irish issue.

New York still had the largest population of Irish-born and those with at least one Irish parent in 1970 with 200,000, followed by Boston with 120,000, and Chicago and Philadelphia with about 70,000 each, while San Francisco and Los Angeles had about 28,000 each.[9] In other cities the representation was scattered, but still identifiable. The Provo partisans knew that this population had certain psychological predispositions. First, there was in it, and especially among those from Northern Ireland, anti-English sentiment that, although subdued before 1969, had been resoundingly activated by the events in Northern Ireland since then. Second, was the characteristic sociability shared by this population. The Irish have not lost that heritage of gregarious association built up in their rural culture over the centuries. They have not lost it in the United States. They can be relied on to rally to a series of events where they may indulge this ethnic vitality of sociability. Third, there was the still viable tradition of what might be termed the "patriot patriarch." There were still old IRA men around. Their deeds were now old legend, but their spirits were animated indeed, and they seethed before the television screens as English troops mauled Irish civilians in ugly roundups. Such men held the respect of the Irish and Irish-Americans and were symbolic figures. Actually, the television and newspaper coverage of Northern Ireland events stimulated and magnified all of these psychological predispositions.

As the Irish in the United States followed the Northern Ireland conflict, day by day and week by week, as they talked about it in bars, kitchens, clubs, and at their jobs, their anger converged on some practical measures. They had to keep informed, somehow provide relief for those in Derry and Belfast burned out of their homes, and try to make the American public aware of the destruction being wrought by British policy.

In the United States the Irish sympathizers knew how flatly the bland English pronouncements contradicted the basic accounts that were reaching them from acquaintances, relatives, and returning American journalists. Irish newspapers gave realistic coverage. The *United Irishman* from Dublin was the Marxist Offical IRA paper, but its circulation in the United States was very limited. In Dublin the Provo IRA had set up its own news bureau, and this sent mimeographed bulletins to American contacts.[10] Some local groups tried to put together photocopy news mock-ups of clippings.

A very important element in the organization of the American network to support the dissidents in Ulster was the *Irish People,* published from 2649 Bainbridge Avenue, the Bronx, New York City. The Irish newspapers in the past had always been precious channels for news of nationalist activity. John Devoy's fiery *Gaelic American* had been the most radical among them. In 1918, when at English request the United States government banned leading Irish papers from the mails, Joseph McGarrity launched and personally subsidized a publication called *The Irish Press.* In 1970 it was clear to the Irish in the United States that English versions of the conflict in the North would get heavy coverage. The press officers of the British army and a broad range of government officials and propaganda specialists ground out news releases, situation reports, interpretive stories, gave background interviews, and plied the wire services and foreign press men with the English side of the issue. Conscious distortion was, of course, a normal government news management technique.

The emergence of the *Irish People* was fitful. Its early editing left much to be desired, but by 1972 it had improved. Pictures, cartoons, a three-color masthead, a letter column, advertisements and report columns from various American cities were added. However, the heart of the paper was the hard news from Ulster. It was frequently lurid news of torture and grisly

details of casualties. Pictures showed blood-drenched bodies. References
and reprints of ballads linked the struggle to the Irish Republican tradition.
Editorials bitterly denounced each week's English and Northern Unionist
blunder or tactic. It was a hard-line paper about a rough war.

The *Irish People* carried extensive information about the activities of
sympathetic groups like the Irish Northern Aid organization. It carried cor-
rective information about sensational incidents, information that did not
appear in American papers. If there was a terrible bombing attributed to
the IRA with allegations that there had been no warning, the *Irish People*
would print excerpts from an English army military log registering the IRA
warning. Coverage of hunger strikers and IRA notables was extensive. These
items attracted a considerable following for the paper in Irish-American
communities. The *Irish People* supplied a vital means of communication
that greatly enlivened the support network.

All through 1970 to 1972 the Irish Northern Aid organization worked
to build its following. Taverns and bars were invaluable places for reaching
potential members. The Irish saloonkeeper had played a historic role in
the political and nationalist organizing of the past, and his function was
just as valid in the 1970s as it had been in the nineteenth century. He took
advertisements in the *Irish People,* made contributions, opened his premises
for gatherings. Clothing donated for those expelled from their homes in
Northern Ireland was collected. The Irish radio programs in larger cities
carried announcements of meetings and fund-raising events. By 1973 a review of the columns of the *Irish People* showed that Irish Northern Aid
branches in Manhattan, Queens, Astoria, Staten Island, and on Long Island
in New York were hard at work. Branches in Connecticut and New Jersey
were active, and those in Washington, D. C., Baltimore, Philadelphia, Boston, Buffalo, Chicago, and St. Louis all holding meetings and events.[11] In
Detroit, the Ancient Order of Hibernians was collaborating with Irish Northern Aid.

A Catholic bishop, in an unusual clerical association with the movement,
appeared in October, 1973, with Provisional spokesman, Ruiairi O'Bradaigh,
who was touring the United States to develop support. This was one of the
few instances in which a churchman openly associated with Provo circles.
As had been true in the past, the more prominent Irish-American businessmen
avoided identification with the controversial IRA sympathizers. Indeed, in
the same issue of the *Irish People* noting Bishop Thomas J. Drury's presence at the October meeting, an editorial appeared under the title, "Lace
Curtains and Hypocrisy" recalling that the American Irish Historical Society
in New York had held a fete honoring Mrs. Patricia Ryan Nixon. The American Irish Historical Society was an old line organization with headquarters
on Fifth Avenue. Notables such as Secretary of Labor Peter Brennan, Con-

servative Senator James Buckley and Cardinal Terence Cooke attended the affair. The *Irish People* bitterly flayed these conservative figures for paying court to Mrs. Nixon, while President Richard Nixon had ignored the Northern Ireland struggle.[12]

In such places as Cleveland, Ohio, groups of Irishmen were hearing visiting IRA speakers tell the Provo story. On the East Side of Cleveland, a group of Irish workers, emigrated from Achill, County Mayo, formed the nucleus of Irish Northern Aid sympathy. In Butte, Montana, where the Irish had gone for generations to work in the copper mines, another group collected funds and sold the *Irish People*.[13] In San Francisco, young Irishmen met with radicals from Berkeley to consider the Irish issue, while in Cambridge, Massachusetts, a bar called "The Plough and the Stars" became a Provo rallying point. As the guerrilla war raged in 1971 and 1972, these groups worked to send money to Ireland and to aid the Provisional IRA in any way they could.[14]

Strangers began to appear in the major cities in 1971, men—usually young— who were practically full-time organizers for Irish Northern Aid. At times they would confess to having recently been ill or having some disability. Other men worked for building contractors or in bars. They gave all of their wages to the various support groups except what they needed for minimal living expenses. These were men on the run, former prisoners recuperating, wanted men recovering from wounds. They were exiled from Northern Ireland but still deeply engaged with the conflict there. Occasionally they would fly to Shannon Airport in the Republic to slip back into the North to see a very ill parent or to attend an IRA funeral for a friend killed in a raid or sniping battle with the English army. These men were walking testimony to the grim commitment involved in the North.

There were abroad also agents of the Marxist Offical wing of the IRA that was only intermittently embroiled in the fighting in the North. These socialist and radical representatives found ready acceptance among Marxists in the United States.They could circulate among certain labor groups, find friends in the Marxist intellectual circles in universities, and appeal to the "New Left" radicals in youth groups. The Marxist IRA supporters would collaborate with the Provisional IRA organizations in rallies and picketing activities, but the gulf between the Provos, usually traditionalist Catholics, and the Marxists was considerable.[15]

Aside from telecasts from Northern Ireland itself and the brief visits of the Rev. Ian Paisley, the Protestant position in the North was not actively presented in the United States. Some said this was so because the Protestant Unionist position was so hard to defend. The Northern leadership did send a "truth squad" to the United States to follow Bernadette Devlin and try to counteract her skillful rhetoric, but the spokesmen of the "truth squad"

turned out to be perfect mannequins of Ulster propriety and as dull as a
Presbyterian Sunday school recitation. It seemed as if the Unionists relied
on British cabinet ministers to argue their case for them, and such figures
as Harold Wilson, Edward Heath, Reginald Maudling, and James Callaghan
were widely quoted in American papers repeatedly, predicting the demise
of the IRA and protesting that London only wanted democracy and peace
in Ulster. The same news stories usually contained accounts of the strenuous
military measures being carried out by armed English forces that eventually
totaled about 30,000, including regular troops, defense auxiliaries, police,
and widespread intelligence cadres.[16]

The moderate opinion in Northern Ireland had been largely outflanked
and intimidated by events after 1969. It took a considerable time for such
opinion to recover and to try to frame a program that aimed at peace and
eventual reconciliation of the warring communities. During 1971, an organization seeking a centrist ground worked to promote support for a Protestant-
Catholic coalition government. This fusion of liberal opinion termed itself
the New Ulster Movement. It had begun in the late 1960s, seeking to lobby
for a new Northern Ireland constitution and power sharing. Its chairman,
Brian Walker, spoke out for reconciliation and new economic and political
terms for Ulster. The Women's Peace Movement, the Alliance Party, and
the Social Democratic and Labor Party all attempted to form a firm, moderate middle ground across the bog of violence. The Social Democratic and
Labor Party came to the fore in 1973, however, as the political vehicle for
non-IRA opinion, and took part in the English-sponsored efforts to build a
power-sharing government in the North after the Stormont government was
suspended. Although the news media in the United States reported these
efforts, the effective Irish community in America paid scant attention to
them. Too much blood had been shed. Too many mistakes had been made.
The proponents of force dominated Irish-American organizations concerned
with the Northern Ireland problem.[17]

The responses of American political figures and government spokesmen
to the Northern Ireland problem were really quite limited. A few leading
politicos sallied forth with statements, but higher officials of the Nixon
administration treated the entire issue as if it were on another planet. Representative William Ottinger (D., N. Y.) declared in August 1970 that the
use of the Special Powers Act that flagrantly abrogated civil rights by the
Northern Ireland government was "the road to tyranny." He decried repression and read into the *Congressional Record* a petition drafted by
Paul O'Dwyer of New York in 1968. This petition requested an investigation by the United Nations Human Rights Commission, with possible im-
position of sanctions against the government of Northern Ireland, be
considered.[18]

Senator Edward Kennedy (D., Mass.) took a strong and reasoned stand on Northern Ireland, and because of his prominence, he earned outraged rejoinders from English publications. In October, 1971, he and Representative Hugh Carey (D., N. Y.) jointly submitted a resolution to Congress. This resolution urged the withdrawal of English troops from Northern Ireland. Kennedy attacked the internment policy and said Ulster was becoming England's Viet Nam. He charged that the Stormont government ruled by "bayonet and bloodshed." He was joined by Senator Abraham Ribicoff (D., Conn.) in denouncing England's policy and Stormont's brutality. Conservative Senator James Buckley urged withdrawal of English troops. Thus, Massachusetts, Connecticut, and New York, all states with significant Irish political traditions, made testimonies of political concern. Secretary of State William P. Rogers responded that "it would be both inappropriate and counterproductive for the United States to attempt to intervene in any way in the area." Up and down the line, the Nixon administration was cold to any move by the United States that would stay England's rough hand in Ulster.[19]

In March 1972 when Prime Minister Edward Heath finally conceded the bankruptcy of the Stormont government and suspended it in favor of direct rule of Ulster from London, Senators Kennedy, Ribicoff, and Congressman Hugh Carey praised the change. *Time* magazine hailed Heath's action. Later Kennedy made a statement to the House Foreign Affairs Subcommittee on Europe. In this statement he urged unification of the English-held Six Counties with the Irish Republic. Martin J. Hillenbrand, Assistant Secretary of State for European Affairs warned the same subcommittee that United States intervention "would not advance the interests of Ireland but could, in fact, set them back."[20]

The Irish groups in the United States soon gathered that the administration of Richard M. Nixon was not about to utter a word in behalf of the beleaguered Protestants and Catholics living under British guns in Ulster. They turned their most diligent efforts to raising funds. If Bernadette Devlin could raise $200,000 for civil rights in 1969, the Irish Northern Aid groups could do better. They did. In 1972, especially, money was raised steadily for relief of burned out families in Belfast and Derry, for support of the families of internees, for medical aid, and the other costs of violence. Money was also raised for arms, to pay for IRA operating expenses, for propaganda to contradict the English press service barrage.

But the full record of assistance to the Catholic minority and to the IRA will ever remain obfuscated. Not all monies going to Ireland flowed through Irish Northern Aid. Much was taken back by returning immigrants. Money given freely with no receipts involved was entirely portable. How much flowed across the Atlantic to support the Provos? A good guess might be half a million dollars in 1972, half that in 1973, much less in 1974.[21] Together with money from England and the Irish Republic, the underground funds fueled the Provo campaign. It bought arms in England and Europe, bribed officials, paid for the gun squads and bombers. The financial picture will ever be obscure, purposely so.

Was it true, as the Marxist Official IRA alleged, that Dublin cabinet ministers paid to set up the Provos to forestall a Socialist growth in Ireland? Perhaps. Was it true that the New York activists alone sent $30,000 a month to the North in 1972? Perhaps. Was it true that Colonel Khadafi of Libya sent substantial funds? Perhaps. The clearest evidence of the input of money is that guns, explosives, and other equipment were at work in Ulster. War, even underground war, costs money. The Provisional IRA had to pay its way like any organization, and it did so with plenty of aid from the network in the United States.

The support network that had grown up since 1969 was composed of the efforts of immigrants, mostly North of Ireland people and those close to them. This made it a relatively small network. It did function in league with a thin web of Irish organizations across the United States though the Irish Northern Aid branches were its backbone. Some new features were a departure from the traditional Irish-American nationalist formula. The youth culture providing some radical allies and the jet plane service that greatly facilitated communications were new additions, as was the powerful sensitizing influence of the mass media and television coverage of the Ulster conflict, at least in the beginning.

The network was militant with a gut motivation, but it was not a rigidly organized system. The Irish characteristic of sociability and traditional antagonism toward England were its great resources. The affluence of the United States made sufficient money available so that even hard-working immigrants could spare enough for contributions to the movement. The work to aid the minority in Northern Ireland was both clandestine and open, but the terror bombing in Ulster and the limitations of the support network's influence precluded capturing the very broad and complex opinion bloc of the mass of Irish-Americans. Nor could the network affect American government policy toward Northern Ireland or England. Deprived of broad support from the Catholic church, American politicians, or wealthy Irish-Americans, the network did what it could do best, maintain its immigrant followers and their close allies, and raise money through a steady but limited cycle of events in cities across the country.

4

TWISTING THE LION'S TAIL

The groups in the United States supporting opposition to England in Ulster revived a time-honored catalog of tactics in their drive to obtain friends and money for their cause. The old fellows still around who remembered the 1920s and the big drive for Irish independence could recite a whole repertoire of agitators' activities. Many of the tactics were standard American lobbying and public relations ploys. Other activities of a more folksy character were long-standing features of Irish community affairs. Most important was the necessity of keeping up a steady and sufficiently heated flow of information. This was aided by the Irish Republican News Service in Dublin, the *Irish People* with its coverage of the Ulster war and politics, and reports to Irish groups of representatives who had recently seen first-hand the barbed wire and daily tension in Northern Ireland.[1]

Local American newspapers were encouraged to carry stories of Irish gatherings and reports of the repression in Ireland. News conferences with special personalities speaking on the problem were held when opportunity offered. Rallies, fund-raising dinners, and interviews with local people from Northern Ireland were given newspaper space. Some of the larger metropolitan dailies sent correspondents to file special stories from Belfast or Derry. Wire service material was, of course, used freely, especially when such events as the fabulous IRA prison escapes took place. Not many newspapers can resist stories of the flight of prisoners out of the jailyard by helicopter or the mass escape of nineteen IRA men through a blown-out prison wall.

In order to keep politicians from ignoring the Northern Ireland issue, letter-writing campaigns were organized. Letters to the editor were a constant reminder to the public that Irish feeling ran high on the subject. Major news events such as the initiation of internment, the killings of civilians in Derry in 1972 by English paratroops, or the suspension of the Stormont government brought flurries of letters to editors. Petitions were circulated, signed, and sent off to congressmen and senators.

Boycotts of English-made goods were organized, and in many an American bar it was a hazardous act to request a Scotch or order Gordon's gin. Some stores in New England had their entire stocks of Cadbury's chocolate smashed by Irish children encouraged by their mothers. The offices of the British Overseas Airways Corporation were regular targets for picketing groups of IRA sympathizers. The British Embassy in Washington and British consulates were picketed regularly. Lapel buttons reading "England Out" or "Support the IRA" were sold and car bumper stickers with slogans like "Bomb Britain" and "Remember the Derry Massacre" appeared. Artifacts and Christmas cards made by prisoners in Northern jails were much sought after. Rubber bullets, tear gas canisters, and other tokens of the Irish violence were displayed, and the point was made that these and practically all the weapons used against the Catholics in the North were from North Atlantic Treaty Organization stocks, and many of them paid for by American taxes.

The chief activity of the support groups, however, was money raising, and this was done at dozens of events monthly. These events were advertised in Irish newspapers, on the Irish radio programs, in fraternal organization newsletters, and most importantly by word of mouth. Mary would arrange to meet her cousin Sheila at the "club" next Saturday. Mary hadn't seen Sheila since the baby was born. Councilman Donaghue would make a note to be sure to be there. The two big lads from Roscommon who worked as telephone linemen would get dates to attend. Sometimes a mailing would be made to Irish club mailing lists:

Report from the North. Direct from Derry. Michael O'Doherty, free after 6 months internment, will speak.

> And the land that calls us homeward
> Can but share with us her tears.
> James Connolly

Refreshments and dancing to the Connaught Ceili Orchestra. 8 - 1 AM. Admission $10.00.[2]

These events were patronized both by families, including children, and by the "singles," unmarried immigrant boys and girls who enjoyed the socializing as well as the expressing of support for the Northern rebels.

Behind these events there flowed a stream of more informal activities. Clothes were sent to relatives whose possessions had been burned in Ulster riots. Children were brought to the United States for visits that might relieve them of the tension of ever-present army surveillance, and to take them out of the temptation to join the street harrassment of soldiers or their Protestant counterparts. Money was sent to aid emigration of relatives out of the North to the Irish Republic, to England, to Australia or Canada. Because of the current quotas for immigration to the United States, the chances of gaining entry were not too good, so other places had to be sought. Loans were made so that cars could be bought to replace those hijacked or burned.

Behind the public events, too, was the more sinister work of smuggling arms to the IRA or to relatives and friends who simply wanted weapons to defend themselves. There is so much weaponry in the United States and so many ways of obtaining and shipping guns and ammunition that it is almost impossible to stop clandestine traffic. There is a whole rural and small town culture in America that thrives on its gun hobbies, and in the cities even high school kids know how to acquire guns and use them. Mail order houses, gunsmiths, pawn shops, illicit gun dealers, returned service-men with "souvenirs," police selling confiscated weapons, sporting goods dealers, and various armed underground fringe groups could all supply arms. From such piecemeal sources, the Irish were able to acquire with a fair de-gree of ease a miscellaneous but still deadly armory for secret shipment to Ulster.

It is appropriate to examine a local branch of the support network to see how it functions in specific terms. The activities of Irish Northern Aid and other groups in Philadelphia provide an opportunity to review the support mechanism. Philadelphia is a city with a long tradition of Irish ties. The Irish are woven into the city's history, and there is a record of over two hundred years of anti-English agitation on the part of the city's Irish community. As with many major cities, the black population has all but totally occupied the older areas that were the nineteenth-century working class districts. As a result, most of the old Irish neighborhoods are now part of the black ghetto. A few areas of Irish-Catholic population remain, but these are small and mingled with Italian and other peoples. For the most part the Irish have dispersed to the outlying neighborhoods and the suburbs. Several of the suburbs themselves have fairly strong Irish histories due to settlement by railroad, mill, or domestic workers who were Irish.[3]

The dispersion of the old Irish population concentrations, however, did not dissolve the Irish social community. This community has adjusted to all kinds of changes. In the nineteenth century, industrialization tended to disperse the community as families followed employment. The automobile age, social mobility, and affluence continued that process. But there was always a tight gathering of recently emigrated families to keep the county societies and beneficial organizations going. The more assimilated Irish-Americans were content to patronize the Society of the Friendly Sons of St. Patrick or the Commodore John Barry Observance Day Committee. The old clubs in the inner city were gradually abandoned, and new halls for dances and events were found in outlying areas.

Economically, the immigrants who sustained the Irish organizations after World War II were largely of working or lower-middle-class status. They were skilled tradesmen, small contractors, or building trades mechanics, tavern keepers or men with small businesses. The girls were often nurses, secretaries, or shop attendents. They tended to be people with strong Irish school training through or beyond the secondary level. They lived in the little Philadelphia brick row houses, worked hard, paid their bills, and viewed the furies and follies of America with the sardonic eyes of canny Irish villagers.

Irish organizations before 1969 were very weak. The county societies numbered only half a dozen. A federation that linked them functioned largely to avoid conflicts in scheduling their affairs. The strongest societies were those composed of people from Derry, Donegal, Tyrone, Cavan, Mayo and Galway, but there were Kerry and Armagh groups as well. The Friendly Sons of St. Patrick, the Ancient Order of Hibernians, various fraternities related by strong Irish ties to religious orders, the Commodore Barry and St. Patrick's Day Observance Committees functioned fitfully. There were still plenty of Irish in Philadelphia city politics, including the first Irish-Catholic mayor of the city, James H. J. Tate, but the tightly administered Archdiocese under Polish-American Archbishop John J. Krol left little room for crusading Irish clergymen. The focus of the Irish community was the Irish Center in racially integrated, middle-class Mt. Airy in the northwest of the city. There were bars and halls in other areas, however, that were regular haunts, and there were center city taverns and restaurants that were favored as well.

In 1969 a group of Friends of the Northern Ireland Civil Rights Association was formed under the energetic leadership of Jack McKinney, a newspaperman and television commentator. Born in South Philadelphia, McKinney was no misty-eyed dreamer of the Emerald Isle. He was a hard-jawed former athlete with direct ties to the North, where he had many friends. He used his television show to publicize the problems and demands of the Ulster civil rights protagonists. Gathering together local activists, he arranged a rally at the University Museum of the University of Pennsylvania in 1969. Flanking the stage were enlarged photographs of former President John F. Kennedy and Rev. Martin Luther King. The attendees were a mixed crowd, Irish immigrants, native Irish-Americans, local university people, representatives of liberal groups, and a few blacks. A handsome black baritone sang

"A Nation Once Again" to strong applause, and Irish musicians played nationalist songs between brief addresses that described the predicament of the Catholic minority in Ulster.

McKinney organized subsequent meetings at the Irish Center, but he was unable to sustain the interest of blacks and liberal groups in maintaining a strong and representative front with the Irish civil rights activists. As the violence in Ireland increased in 1971 and 1972, the following developed by McKinney became less diverse and more Irish. The blacks had their own staggering problems, and the Jews were increasingly worried about Israel. American-born people of Irish background were usually confused by the complex and contradictory nature of the Ulster situation, and if they had no direct interests involved, such as relatives there, they tended to give up their attention in the face of the muddle of contention and violence.

There were some academic people deeply interested in the problem because they had family ties to Ireland, because they had studied or written about the island, or because they had pursued graduate studies there. A few were proponents of IRA violence, but most were fairly objective analysts of the situation, though they had Irish nationalist sympathies. A law student at the University of Pennsylvania organized a meeting attended by numerous faculty and students. The meeting was addressed by Billy McMillen, long-time Belfast leader of the Official IRA. A teacher at Villanova University taught a sixteen-week course entirely devoted to the Northern Ireland issue. The James Larkin Irish Republican Club arranged a seminar on the issue at LaSalle College. Other local colleges had speakers and programs address the issue in 1971 and 1972. Those with academic ties, however, were only remotely related to the Irish clubs that were becoming increasingly active with respect to the North.

In August of 1969 Bernadette Devlin visited Philadelphia, and the Irish did something they hadn't done for years. They rented a huge ballroom in a downtown hotel. On the evening of the Devlin appearance they almost filled it, too. The crowd was enthusiastic as Miss Devlin tore into the Unionist junta of the North. It was delighted when she sang a song in Irish in a surprisingly lovely voice. Miss Devlin's socialist formulas and her solidarity with American blacks, however, somewhat cooled local Irish support for her, and it was notable that a reception given for her prior to the speech was studiously avoided by most of the local Irish judges, wealthy contractors, and political leaders.

In 1969 the *Evening Bulletin,* the *Philadelphia Inquirer* and the *Philadelphia Daily News* all carried headline coverage of Ulster's crisis, and this coverage continued. Jack McKinney went to Northern Ireland and filed stories for the *Daily News.* One of the *Evening Bulletin*'s top reporters, Peter Binzen, went to Ireland and filed a feature series on the struggle. A black columnist for the *Daily News,* Chuck Stone, wrote a number of columns identifying Ulster Catholic problems with similar problems of American blacks. John Corr of the *Philadelphia Inquirer* also filed a series of pieces from Ulster. Radio station call-in shows and interview panels devoted programs to the subject.[4]

Congressman William Green, a young and attractive Democrat, agreed to head a branch of the American Committee for Ulster Justice, the nonpartisan and non-sectarian group based in New York.[5] In 1972 this group held meetings with local college students to explain the Ulster tangle, distribute book lists and literature, and publicize the need for interreligious activity for pacification of the Northern Ireland cauldron.

During 1971 the local Irish organizations began to increase their activities for the North. Although weekly meetings of various groups were held at the Irish Center, a number of taverns and outlying locations were also centers for events featuring speakers and for fund-raising gatherings. Every time a major incident took place in Ireland, or a local paper tried to sort out some editorial position on the troubles there, a spate of letters would flow into the newspapers. The *Irish People* and the *United Irishman* began to be sold at downtown newsstands and bars around the city.

In January 1972 Jack McKinney arranged a press conference for Mrs. Margaret Murray, a Belfast resident whose two sisters had been slain by English troops as they drove through the streets of their city. Mrs. Murray's brother had been beaten terribly by troops during internment. McKinney devoted several columns in the *Daily News* to Mrs. Murray's story, and these articles produced outrage in the Irish community. Mrs. Murray's family had been subjected to tragedy that she recounted on a local television program with an extraordinary dignity and grave self-containment. The impression she made was heart-scalding to Irish-Philadelphians, and it prompted many to pledge themselves to do something to retaliate against the army that could act so savagely against civilians.[6]

By 1972 an active local network was functioning in behalf of Irish Northern Aid. Joe McCaffrey, Irish-born and from a strong Republican family, led a branch of the organization in Northeast Philadelphia.[7] Other branches grew up in the Olney area, Upper Darby, and around the Irish Center. Branches in adjacent counties and in New Jersey were formed. All held fund-raising parties, dances, and picnics. An advertisement in the *Daily News* on June 21, 1972, listed nine branches and stated that the aims of the groups were:

1. A new free Ireland based on four regional provincial governments.
2. A new broad-based Irish constitution guaranteeing equal rights to all citizens.
3. An end to all violence in Ireland.

4. A general amnesty for all held on political charges.
5. A complete withdrawal of British troops.
6. A program of restitution financed by England to aid the Irish economy.

The advertisement also criticized English actions in Ireland and recalled that America was founded by people who found English rule intolerable.

The *Philadelphia Magazine* carried an article describing IRA fund raising that included a benefit honoring one of the Irish patriarchs of the city. The affair was organized by the toughest labor union in town, John McCullough's roofers. When John McCullough collected money, he meant it, and the returns were said to be high. McCullough was a much-decorated former marine of incredibly tough physique, and the kind of man who would delightedly spit in the face of an English paratroop officer just for provocation.[8]

Picketing was a regular activity of the Irish partisans.[9] Groups staged a "sit-in" at the British Consul's office, and picketed the British Overseas Airways Corporation repeatedly. These picket lines, replete with signs, included old and young activists, men, women, and children, and drew considerable attention from downtown crowds. One evening a Main Line dowager in glittering gown alighted from her chauffer-driven limousine in front of the august Academy of Music. It was bitter cold, and she drew her furs around her, then recoiled in horror. The pavement in front of the Academy throbbed with the tramp of pickets. The London Symphony was playing that night. The dowager approached a ruddy-faced little man in the line wrapped in "bawneen" woolen sweaters with an old cap crammed on his head.

"What are you doing here?" she demanded.

"Me brother's been lifted, Ma'am," the man yelled at her belligerently. "Me own brother's locked in a Limey prison camp!"

The lady gazed around in bewilderment a moment, looked behind her to see if her car was there. It was gone. She caught up to the little man, borrowed his sign, and joined the freezing pickets.

Quakers in Philadelphia sent observers and peace workers to Ireland. Helen Campbell, who worked in Derry to aid families of internees, came to Philadelphia and spoke of the harrowing conditions in which she worked. The Official IRA was actively represented in picketing and speaking on campuses. Some Philadelphia priests visited Ulster, but returned pessimistic about the restoration of peace.

In late 1972 Dr. Michael Hurst, a historian, of Oxford University gave a lecture at Villanova University. He airily chattered on about the North of Ireland, witty, seemingly pleased with his opportunity to pursue that venerable English academic indulgence, instructing the Americans. During the question period, he was mauled furiously, especially by one John McGee. The rather pompous Hurst was asked, "Why are so very few Protestants interned?"

"They have no history of terrorism," he replied. The audience roared.

McGee asked, "How do you know the Catholics interned are terrorists since they've never been tried?"

Dr. Hurst replied, "It is not necessary to place specific charges against internees under the Special Powers Act." The audience howled. John McGee earned his living as a gardener.

Early in 1972 a reporter for the *Evening Bulletin* estimated that $10,000 a month was being raised for the Northern Ireland dissidents in Philadelphia.[10] These funds were the result of proceeds from dances and rallies, contributions from Irish organizations, collections taken up in bars and contributions from individuals. One old fellow, a native of County Clare, took up collections almost full time. Contributors received a card as a receipt with two lines printed on it:

> "Though the strife of the North fill poor Erin with care,
> There are hearts true and trusted toward Erin so fair."

Owen B. Hunt, Sligo-born IRA veteran and life-long Irish activist, had excerpts from the press concerning Northern Ireland reprinted and circulated at his own expense. Dennis Cassin, organizer for Irish Republican Clubs, printed a newsletter to gather support in his Kensington mill district. A complement to the fund raising was the distribution of inexpensively reprinted propaganda materials: speeches by Senator Edward Kennedy; Freedom Petitions; Affidavits of people interned and tortured; medical reports on torture victims; statements by the representatives of the Irish Republic at the United Nations; statements from Amnesty International and the International League of Jurists; and Provisional IRA materials on the future of the North such as the pamphlet *Eire Nua* (New Ireland).

There was considerable diversity of opinion about the solutions proposed for the North among Philadelphia Irishmen. All would condemn England's blundering and exploitation of the problem over the years and the brutality since 1969. But many did not believe that Ulster was Ireland's pre-eminent problem. Many despised the Irish Republic's leaders as bourgeois frauds and would agree with Ruairi O'Bradaigh's remarks to a Philadelphia audience that those leaders "ignored the plight of the northern Irish" and "collaborated with the British."[11] Others thought that the whole problem had to be seen in the perspective of the neo-colonial domination of all of Ireland that bartered away natural resources, maintained stagnant church-run education, high emigration, and an exploitative set of upper class privileges. The solutions for the North, however, were complex and too long-range to command general consensus. It was the immediate problems of a repressive English army, torture, stumbling English prescriptions for an Ulster government, and bitter contempt for the Unionist power brokers that commanded consensus. On these things the Irish agreed, though not all worked for the Provo support network.

The round of fund-raising events continued very actively through 1972 and into 1973. Church halls were used for the appearance of such speakers as Father Sean McManus. Seamus McCaffrey, Brendan Sullivan, Mrs. Maureen Garvin, Brendan McCusker and dozens of others worked eagerly to keep the roster full of activities in the city and suburbs. Frank McManus, Member of Parliament for Fermanagh-South Tyrone, spoke at the Church of the Incarnation Hall.[12] A rally in sympathy with four men jailed in Fort Worth Texas for Irish activities was held at Independence Square where 200 people heard John McGee speak. Patrick White wrote to the *Philadelphia Inquirer* to praise Senator Edward Kennedy's plea for peace in Ulster.[13] Joe McCaffrey urged that IRA followers buy T-shirts with IRA lettering and symbols on them, and these soon appeared on work sites, ball fields, and boys' clubs all over the city.

In May 1973 the Irish partisans were shaken by an action of the United States Justice Department. Three local men were subpoenaed by a Federal grand jury investigating aid to Northern Ireland. Daniel Duffy, Neil Byrne, and Daniel Cahalane were all summoned to testify. Federal attorneys said the three men were to be questioned about aid to the IRA. Lawyers for the three men claimed the phones of the Irishmen had been tapped. The Irish activists in the area reacted with raging invective. The Nixon administration was wallowing in tangles of corruption that nobody seemed to be able to unravel, yet the Justice Department had sent lawyers into Philadelphia to harass people aiding their relatives against English persecution. Pickets charged in front of the Federal Courthouse on May 9 with signs saying "British Terrorist Regime Enlists Support of U. S. Justice Department to Stop Aid to Oppressed People of Northern Ireland."[14] It would be hard to exaggerate the fury, disgust, and contempt for the Nixon government that this affair aroused among the Philadelphia Irish.

Daniel Cahalane, a small contractor, was soon made the focus of the Federal efforts. He was suspected of buying $20,000 worth of guns and ammunition in nearby Norristown, Pa. Mr. Cahalane refused to answer grand jury questions, for he believed that his civil rights would not be protected under grand jury procedures. On July 27, 1973, he was jailed for contempt of the grand jury. At first he was denied bail in a peculiarly vindictive move by the Federal authorities.[15] On appeal, Judge Arlin Adams permitted release on bail. A Defense Fund was formed to aid Cahalane's family and help pay legal fees. Barney McTeague, Liam Henify, and Maureen Garvin worked diligently for it. In October, 1973, Paul O'Dwyer came to the city from New York on the day before his own crucial city election to speak on behalf of Cahalane. "We would be well off in this country," he said, "in using the forces of law and order to snuff out abuses of the courts and not using them to persecute those fighting for freedom and justice like Dan Cahalane. . . . He has been imprisoned because the grand jury has been used time after time in this country as an instrument of persecution by the government. . . . If this man is guilty of a crime, then charge him before a jury of his peers. But it is not right to send him to prison without a fair trial."[16] To those who had witnessed the Agnew-Nixon drives to suppress dissent, O'Dwyer's remarks seemed patently true.

5

THE MILITANT MIND

In the face of social isolation in American life and the imputation of guilt for the violence visited on Northern Ireland through support for the guerrilla movement, the partisans of the Provisional IRA would seem to have had a problem of conscience. Coming from a highly moralistic Roman Catholic tradition, they are forced to reconcile their association with conspiracy, violence, and insurrection with the Gospel that they hear preached on Sundays in their Catholic churches. It is clear from the outset of any conversation with those who support the Provisionals, however, that the long history of ambiguity in Christianity about violence is well known to them. They are not about to concede that the Irish are more violent than others, or that any Irish struggle is somehow more of a contradiction of moral values than the struggles of other people. What they do see as characteristic of the Irish problem is a scandalous one-sidedness, with a mighty England ranged against the aspirations of a small people.

In order to better try to understand the outlook of supporters of the Provisional IRA I have spent considerable time in conversation with a sample of these supporters. In bars, at Irish social affairs, in homes and in other settings, I have listened to them as intently as I could.[1] I have tried to record their sentiments accurately and weigh them against the views of people I know who still live in Ulster or the Irish Republic. I have concluded that the views of the Irish-American supporters for the Provisional IRA are not too different from those of Provo supporters in Ireland in the roots of their argument and the depth of their feelings. The American contingent is somewhat less realistic about the problems involved in Ulster, somewhat behind in the range of information available, but not too far afield from the Irish in Ireland in outlook, given the individual commitment to Provisional

IRA orientation. Of course, and this must be strongly emphasized, there are in all walks of Irish life, and in all segments of the Irish-American group, a clear majority of people who do *not* share the Provisional IRA commitment. Among those who *do,* the commitment runs deep.

There does not seem to be a single personality type supporting the Provisional IRA. I have spoken to old and young, voluble and taciturn, sentimental and realistic. Within the range of occupational and social characteristics previously noted in this book, many different types of people defend the Provo position. The following is a selection of people with whom I have had extended discussions of the Northern Ireland problem and the violent events since 1969.

Jimmy O.—This man is about 33. He has worked in Ireland, England, and Panama. He is currently a building construction worker. He is strong and able. He is aggressively outspoken about the Provos and will go out of his way to talk on the subject. He comes from a tough IRA family, several members of which have "done time" in prison in Ireland for IRA work. Because of his family connection, Jimmy says he would support the IRA and especially the more militant wings of it "if we had to stand on the last rock in the world and fight with the last tatter of our souls." He believes that James Connolly's Irish Republic of social justice has never been fulfilled, and he believes the Northern Ireland English-oriented power bloc is one of the chief obstacles. The other is the ruling group in Dublin, that he conceives to be "a pack of London bankers' lackeys." Jimmy has no problem justifying the Ulster violence. He wants it to spread in a "war of liberation" for all of Ireland.

Eileen D.—This girl is a waitress in one of the city's fashionable restaurants. Her family has suffered terribly directly and indirectly as a result of the Northern Ireland government. She stresses that they are pious and extremely hard working, but have been the victims of employment and housing discrimination, unemployment, tuberculosis, contemptuous treatment and, frequently, exile as a result of their hard life in Derry. She is not "pious" as they are. She wants an "eye for an eye and a tooth for a tooth." The only way to deal with the rulers of the North, according to Eileen, is to ravage them as they have ravaged her own people, the Irish Catholics. It will be a long struggle, "but it has ever been so." Justice comes hard in Ireland. Does she regret the children bombed to death? She is a mother. She does regret it, and has wept to read of it. "My own children may die in that struggle if they go to live there, she says. But she will not relent in her fierce resolve to subvert the Northern Ireland ruling group whom she sees as consummate bigots immune to any pleas for political or social justice. "Perhaps I am now as hating as they are. So be it. I would go to my grave, then, strangling them." Eileen gives of her small wages to groups she hopes will aid the Provisional IRA.

John and Patricia McQ.—John has lived in America for twenty years and is a naturalized citizen. He and Patricia have five children. In the United States Army he was an explosives expert. His wife is American born of Irish parents. They have held themselves aloof from direct involvement with IRA supporters, yet they deeply sympathize with friends who are directly involved. They attend Irish Northern Aid functions but do not support violence as such. They would like to see a political solution to the Northern issue, but they have been in Ireland enough to believe that the Northern Protestants will not willingly make a pact with Ulster Catholics. John was born in the West of Ireland and knows the limitations of Irish life. He has lived in England and is not stridently anti-English but loathes the London government. He and his wife believe there is an Irish tradition of nationalist effort that is good and must be sustained, although they are fearful of the Northern Ireland problem. It is "like a pit that could suck the whole island into calamity." John says, "Many people thought of the North as the most advanced part of the island because it was more industrialized, had better land and schools and so on. It is really the ultimate bog hole. The Ulster Protestants pride themselves on being different from the 'bog men' of my country, buy they are the most narrow, benighted, politically naïve and stupidly obstructionist crowd in the island." John says the IRA would love to use his talents as an explosive man, but "What use is it? You can't bomb sense into one million fools. Tolerance may come to Ulster, but for my part if it fell into the sea tomorrow I wouldn't blink."

Liam McN.—Liam is a musician. Born in Northern Ireland, he supplements his income as an office worker by playing at dances and Irish concerts. He is fond of playing and does so with gifts that make him renowned locally for his renditions of folk songs. Liam plays the rebel songs that are a major part of the corpus of Irish music. Once a young man asked if he played "peace" songs as well, songs such as those popularized by the anti-war protesters during the Viet Nam war. Liam responded instantly that no real Irish musician would play such songs while other Irishmen were being thrown into English jails in Ulster. Liam sees the conflict in Ulster as one of practical grievances and also as one of a crippled Irish nation seeking to liberate itself from the tentacles of English power that is backed by conglomorate businesses and NATO militarists. He has lived in Dublin and feels the elite there are self-serving exploiters. "Everywhere in every time, the poor get the short end. Well, in the North and anywhere else they choose, it is to be expected that they should refuse to suffer quietly. If this means they kill others, then that is the lesson yet to be learned by men who run governments for their own well-being and neglect the slum children in the alleys of Belfast, Armagh, and Derry."

Peter F.—This man is 81 years of age. He was born in the West of Ireland in a mud cabin where "if you sat close enough to the turf fire to stay warm, the fire would burn your shins. I've the scars of that yet." Peter has taken part in a long series of Irish nationalist endeavors on both sides of the Atlantic. He did dangerous work in England for a secret Irish society in the days before 1921. His views on the North are strident. "That pack of self-righteous jackals that ruled with fascist tyranny in Belfast for fifty years deserves every bit of blasting that they get. Not only should the English soldiers be shot on sight, but their Orange dogs in the bargain. If there is no way to cripple that black crowd, then the whole of Ulster should be laid waste. It can be restored at a later time. Shatter it, burn it and them in it. It was the likes of them that laid waste the rest of Ireland for the privilege to be pet dogs to English exploiters.

"When I think of what my own family suffered from the misrule of England, what heartbreak and misery, I have no mercy on the Ulster Defense Association and the like. What of the children killed? Indeed, the children of Ireland have been murdered in one way or another for generations. Do I regret that toll? I have wept myself dry with it all of a lifetime. I've been to more goddam funerals of people killed in the Irish struggle for nationhood than I can count. Did the English regret the children killed when they fire bombed their Nazi enemies in Dresden? Not likely. Yes, I do regret that keening for children in the North, but it just makes me more bitter that the sacrifice has to be made to dislodge that flock of parasites from the Six Counties.

"If you ask me what would become of the million Orangemen in the North if the IRA won, I'll tell you. They'd be given a choice: live with us in peace or get out. Some say you can't throw out people who've been in a country for three hundred years. My people were in Ireland for three times three hundred years and we were driven from the land like cattle. My father used to say they'd have sent us off in bottomless boats if they could have."

Vincent O.—This man is middle-aged, a former United States marine, a former newspaperman, now a minor official in a government agency. "All wars are gangster work. All wars murder children. There is no clean war. If you tell me about the IRA killing the innocent, I'll tell you about some of the lovely allies of the United States like Franco, Battista and a few other monsters. If I give money to support the Provos, at least I get to pick the enemy in a more specific way than I do when I give my money through taxes to the Defense Department which plays gangster for various oil companies, fruit companies, and bandit governments all over the world. Once you've decided that wars are necessary, you swallow a lot more. I learned that in the Marine Corps." This man has relatives in Northern Ireland whose lives have been threatened both by Protestant militants and soldiers of the British Army.

John O'L.—"Let me tell you about the IRA," says John, who is a gasoline station operator. "They are not fools. There may be fools among them, I know, but they don't operate as fools. I know enough of them to know that they make terrific sacrifices in what they do. That's what I support, those sacrifices. They have had to burn and bomb and shoot just like I did in World War II. We didn't like it, but we did it because we knew it had to be done. They don't have armored cars, electronic sensors, all the money of England at their backs. They run on a belief in what they're doing, most of them.

"The people in Dublin are fat and content. They'd be scared to death to have to deal with the Northern Protestants as part of a united Ireland. The Prods are very sharp and they'd expose all the sweet deals that the Dublin thieves have going, like the Aer Lingus (Irish Airlines) hotel investments and the Irish Hospital Sweepstakes racket. Man, dear, the Prods would tie into all that with holy-go-pious righteousness. Dublin would shake apart overnight. But, the IRA crowd are not afraid of that. They'd love to clean the stables, and I'm for them till they bury me beside me father in old Donegal."

Cornelius F.—has a thriving tavern in a working class neighborhood. "My old man was wild against the IRA. He was a pub keeper in Tyrone, and though he was a Catholic, he was a peace man in the 1920s. The IRA made it so hot for him in the home place that he came here. My mother took me back later. Over the years, I came to see that the old man was wrong, just dead wrong. There's no hope for Tyrone Catholics but to push over the Orange system.

"The Provisionals do kill bystanders, but not so much as the papers say. The papers are set against them. But the Provos also get killed. They do things at tremendous risk to keep faith with one another. Look at the helicopter escape from jail in Dublin. Look at the rescue attempt in the hospital in Belfast. They've got more balls per man than the whole goddam lot of Brits together. They're the only real Irishmen alive. They're not begging tourist tips or gluing together Japanese radios at some plant in Limerick. They're out trying to build the nation that was left unbuilt by the sellout in the 1920s."

John R.—This man is now in his seventies and is a successful small business-man. He was a friend of many who took part in the Irish fighting of the 1920s. He is American-born, but has all his adult life been a member of Irish Republican clubs. "What do I think of the Provisional IRA? If I was just twenty years younger I'd be out with a gun with them myself. Is this extremism, to want that country united and to complete what so many have struggled and died for? I can disagree with their tactics, but never with their commitment to the big goal."

Patrick L.—This man is also in his older age, but still vigorous in business and Irish affairs. "Tell me what group that forced the issue with England that was not considered a bunch of madmen and terrorists." He spits the last word. "Fenians were terrorists. Land Leaguers were terrorists. Pearse, MacDermott, Connolly, all branded terrorists in their day. Then when they're dead and buried and people are living with the benefits of what they won, then they're heroes. Well, I'm for live heroes, not dead ones, and 'Slainte!' ('Health!') to the lads that are at it today. They've done more in the last five years to pull down the Union Jack in the North than anybody did in the last fifty. More power to them!"

Margaret McE.—A woman who has worked as a maid for well-to-do families, she is now middle-aged, single, with brothers on farms in South Armagh. "I've no faith in partition or power sharing or any other thing than fighting them. The Irish people voted in 1918 for a whole, unified country. It was an overwhelming vote for a new, free Ireland. England sabotaged the will of the people. Now the devil is getting his due. 'Up the Provos!' I say."

Seamus D.—is an engineer, Irish-born. He supports the IRA Provisionals, "but not in all things." "I would live in peace with any man, but not the Stormont storm troopers. They are diseased into thinking that they are God's chosen people. I'm not religious. Religion is garbage. Anybody lording it over another group in the name of religion deserves to be bombed. That goes for the Catholics, too. I'm for people, period, and to hell with religion.

"I know the North, I've worked there. The ones with the best land and the good jobs have it lovely. They've got slavey Bridget and slavey Mike to work for them for a pittance. Well, no more. The slaveys have seen the light. There are no minority rights up there, only what suits the top dogs. The only way to break up that system of armed and Bible-bound arrogance is to shoot it apart.

"You hear the English whining about people in the States sending money and guns. It would make you vomit. Those bastards have 30,000 troops in there all told, armed with every piece of hardware science can produce. Why shouldn't I help the Provos when they're up against the like of that?"

Mrs. O'N.—is a cashier in a food market. She goes to college at night "to better herself." "My brother was 'lifted' in August of 1970. They beat him so bad he's blind in one eye. He had no connection with any politics. None. He was a writer, or tried to be, but very much to himself. He worked in a shirt factory. When they let him out fourteen months later, he was Provo all the way. 'I've one good eye yet to sight a gun,' he told me.

"Now I'm not for killing kids and that, but it is a war. A lot of the things laid at the door of the IRA are done by the Limeys themselves or are done by teenage nuts. I know; I have met the IRA men in my home place. I know them and what they are. They're not perfect and mistakes are made, but I tell you, if I was living in my mother's house there, I know there would be no protection whatsoever were it not for the IRA. Look at 'Bloody Sunday.' That's a bit of a clue as to how the British army values Irish lives."

Luke D.—This man is young and is a grammar school teacher. He feels keenly about the Ulster violence. He has many family ties with Derry and thinks of the place as a "colonial zoo kept by the masters in London, a sort of pen for the Irish 'Bantus'." The religious issues involved are seen by him to be diversionary. "I don't think religion means a damn in relation to the problems of Ulster. It is a guise for all kinds of crookedness there. Religion as a source for personal values is real. As a means of proposing social and political solutions or sorting out the issues in Northern Ireland, it is a joke. The people there take religion seriously personally up to the point of community affairs, but after that in politics or in social issues, it is a mockery. They use it as a source of allegiance for every kind of hypocrisy ever invented.

"I support the IRA because they are radical and would, I hope, sweep all that bullshit about the religions of the area into the ocean. If they have to kill to relieve the area of the curse of religious tyranny, then that must be done. Would they supplant Protestant tyranny by Catholic tyranny? Some would try. Others would fight them. I know which side I'd be on. The Irish people must be forced to cast off the idiot superstitions of the churches. The IRA is the chief way to do this. Personal religion is alright like we have in the United States, but religion in politics is poisoning to the life of the [Irish] people."

Mrs. V.—"I went to school in the North. Never a word of Irish history right through secondary school, except some slight bits. Nonsense about the King and all that tripe. My brother and I are split on this issue. He is anti-IRA. I'm for them. They're the last hope for the ghettos of the North.

Nobody in Dublin, London, Washington gives a damn for them. Well, it's up to themselves then. They've got to make a place for themselves in Ulster. The crowd on top won't listen. They're deaf. Well, the bombs will be heard. "My brother says that it's a hopeless war. All wars are that way. Who knows who will win. You have to take your chances. You can't predict. All you can do is hope and act for your cause. One day John Kennedy was master of the world, the next he was dead, and the same with his brother. Who'd have bet on the Algerians or on the Viet Namese, with their bamboo sticks and rockets they couldn't aim? Can you gamble with lives? What else is worth gambling with when the stakes are high? The stakes are high in the North. I am a woman, but I am as much a soldier as the men in Long Kesh on this issue. England out!"

A good example of the Irish minority mentality in operation occurred in Philadelphia in December 1975, at a meeting to hear a speaker on the IRA. The speaker was J. Bowyer Bell, a research associate of Columbia University's Institute of War and Peace Studies. Bowyer Bell is the author of *The Secret Army: The IRA, 1916-1970* which made his visit a subject of considerable interest to many Irish in Philadelphia. Mr. Bowyer Bell appeared at the Commodore Barry Club. An audience of about one hundred had assembled to hear him, but the meeting got off to a poor start. Mr. Bowyer Bell had brought a film he had made about the Provisional IRA, but the film projector was balky. He filled in by making some introductory remarks. He adopted a somewhat avuncular attitude and discussed the Ulster issue in a dispassionate way. Perhaps because of his status as an expert, this approach was interpreted as being patronizing by most of the audience. That soured the initial atmosphere.

After the ably-photographed and edited film was shown depicting the violence in Ulster and the IRA role, Mr. Bowyer Bell again took the floor. Among other things he said that the Provisional IRA was politically naïve and lacked a strong political program, and this was one of its disabilities. He recounted conversations he had in South Armagh and events involving IRA action units. Several persons in the audience were from South Armagh. They took strong exception to the remarks that the Provisional IRA lacked a political program, citing the *Eire Nua* (New Ireland) scheme for a four-province Ireland without any partitioning border or English presence. Mr. Bowyer Bell was not impressed.

When an aged man rose to tell of his recollections of the beginnings of partition in Ireland in the 1920s, Bowyer Bell cut him off rather abruptly. A young Irish engineer remonstrated heatedly with Bowyer Bell for this, saying "Age must be respected." The crowd applauded. Questions kept coming, and Bowyer Bell drew a hostile response from a number of questione some of them loudly profane, for his lofty analysis of the Ulster issue. This was a gut issue for many of those present, and they would not stand for a dispassionate approach that consigned the British, Northern Protestants and Northern Catholics to a mutual plane of mechanical struggle to be interpreted with sophisticated theories of guerrilla warfare. It was their Ireland, their struggle, their people and tradition that was being discussed, and they were outraged by Bowyer Bell's objective stance. At work also was the culture gap between the professorial speaker in his jacket and vest, and the more informally dressed members of the audience. They had a hard time believing that a man like Bowyer Bell, for all of his knowledge and writings, could really get to the heart of an issue that was especially knotted in their own hearts.

It seems clear from the statements cited that the people speaking are intelligent enough to use a variety of information to justify their support for the IRA. The chief assumption underlying all of their assertions is that England has no right to govern any portion of Ireland. The most frequently cited reasons for this premise are that English government in Ireland has been a calamity historically, that the Irish people overwhelmingly rejected that government in 1918, and that the Northern Ireland state is a contrived English fixture and stubborn instrument of colonialism.

History and tradition in a strongly nationalist version are readily brought to the defense of the IRA by its supporters. Their historical knowledge is gross and truncated, but they are convinced of its conclusions. They feel powerfully, emotionally, a living link with the IRA of the 1920s. They sing of it, know its heroes by heart, and idealize its role in Irish history. Their families are often linked to this history, and family tradition is compelling for most. Compelling, too, is the sense of direct grievance, passed on by parents or perhaps personally experienced. The problems of Northern Ireland have been felt by the speakers, and they attribute them all—from unemployment to internment—to the malignant will of the ruling group in Ulster.

Religion does not seem to be a problem for these speakers in the sense that it is difficult for them to reconcile support for the IRA with their personal codes of belief. Most interpret religion in a personal sense, but see little social dimension to it that would provide solutions for Ulster. Most accept religious institutions, but as static elements, not dynamic ones. Religion for most is just one more element in nationalism, and far from the most important.

There is a clear fatalism about the Ulster conflict in the remarks of these people. They see it as ordained by history. They have no faith in partition schemes, power sharing or short-range government formulas. They believe that the rulers of Ulster ordained struggle for the Catholics and now must live with it or yield. They see no guarantee or even concession of minority rights by the English sponsored rulers. Most want no such guarantee. They believe their claim to full power in the North is prior and historically just, but must be confirmed by arms.

The opinions of the nationalist IRA supporters also reveal a simplistic viewpoint that is intolerant of considerations of future political structures, the fate of the Protestant population, the problems ending partition would mean for Dublin. The militant mentality is willing to work all this out later. Hope is the great nostrum. They have a strong prejudice against politics, feeling that political considerations and economic privilege traduced the Republic declared in 1916 and left partition to bedevil future generations.

Finally, the views of these speakers are, I believe, personalist. They gain support from comradeship with others of like mind, but almost all those with whom I have talked would be strong in their opinions even without much group support. They have been schooled in Irish nationalism and it is part of their being. If they are relatively isolated from broad support in the mainstream of American or even Irish opinion, this is not fundamentally disturbing to them. Their cause has many examples of similar isolation, and they know them. These commentators on Ulster's troubles, far from being the gregarious bombasts so commonly assumed to control the Irish-American network, are flinty characters with a fairly simple personal credo of nationalist beliefs. The beliefs are nonideological in that they do not represent any coherent social philosophy or broader picture of the world as it might be. The concern of the IRA supporters is limited to their war with Ulster rulers, though some are revolutionary enough to want to bring down the Dublin government as well.

The expressions in this chapter are, I believe, fairly presented samples of the opinions one hears among Irish people sympathetic to the Provisional IRA. Frequently there were less articulate people present when the opinions I have presented were expressed, and almost always they agreed with the speaker. The Irish love talk and it is not hard to gather opinions such as the above, but it may be extremely difficult to go further and pry into the personal roles people play in the support network.

I have had the opportunity to talk also with persons sympathetic to and supportive of the Official or Marxist wing of the IRA, which has largely abstained from the broad campaign of violence in the North. These partisans are much more likely to cite the labor union radical James Connolly, shot by the British in 1916, and to interpret the Ulster issue in the vocabulary of Marxist and socialist terms used by Bernadette Devlin McAliskey. Supporters of the Official IRA tend to be better educated and to link the Ulster issue more to Third World struggles for liberation than to personal or family grievances.

I do not believe that any amateur psychological speculations by this writer concerning the mentality revealed by these statements would be appropriate. Such speculation based on such a limited view of the personalities represented would be tendentious at best. It suffices to record that the personalities involved in support for the IRA mean what they say in a deeply personal sense, and take actions based on their belief. Their views represent the nationalism of a simpler era in many respects, although the urgency of the present impinges. They are a testimony not only to the dynamic traditions current in Ireland, but to the animation of those traditions among Irish partisans in the United States.

6

COUNTER FORCES

The shock that ran through the Philadelphia branches of Irish Northern Aid when Daniel Cahalane and his friends were hauled before a Federal grand jury was not shared by the hard-core of militants who were at the center of the support network. They were not susceptible to shock. They knew that repression was the lot of their friends in Ulster and that terror was a key tactic in the hurricane of horror gripping the North. They knew that England would put pressure on Washington to stifle the support network in the United States. Several cases similar to that of Daniel Cahalane had alerted the Irish leadership to the fact that the orders were out to cripple their work.

As early as 1970 agents of the Federal Bureau of Investigation had been seeking information in various cities. The FBI, as official custodian of the nation's political super-conscience, and also as the agency in charge of political paranoia, had checked the IRA along with other dissenting groups in its vast files. The original fear, dating far back to World War II, was that the Irish rebels would deal with anybody to get at England. Sean Russell had toured the United States for the IRA in 1939 before he went to Germany to seek aid from the Nazis. In the 1960s it was the Marxist tilt of the Dublin IRA that kept the FBI mildly interested. Many of the FBI agents themselves came from Irish-American families, and their Irish-Catholic credentials made them fine recruits in the days of raving Cold War anti-Communism. Rarely, however, were these men acquainted with Ireland in a direct way. Their Irish Catholicism was quite conservative. They were poles apart from the IRA types. Their Irishry was of the sentimental, nostalgic kind that the British believed to be the source of their troubles in the United States. Ironically, the FBI's Irish-American agents fitted the English stereotypes, but were anti-IRA. The hard men of the support network had little in common with these college-bred careerists of the Federal bureaucracy.

In 1970 in various cities the FBI made clumsy efforts to snuggle up to the IRA supporters. Usually some pretense of sympathy accompanied the effort. Agents with fake old country accents would call known activists, but the wily Irish at the other end of the phone would soon know that the approach was not bona fide. The FBI apparently abandoned this tactic. Other Federal agencies were alerted to be on the lookout for fugitives wanted by the British. The United States is not Ulster, however, and tracking down illegal immigrants, men gaining entrance on tourist and student visas, and other birds of passage is a frustrating task in a country of mass mobility. The Immigration and Naturalization Service was soon busy along with the FBI in the Federal effort to disrupt the support network. The United States Customs Bureau was alert for arms smuggling; the Internal Revenue Service was out to trip up illegal fund raising; and local and state police were tied into the Federal information system—all joined the quest for IRA activists.

It is notable that this Federal activity burgeoned after Prime Minister Theodore Heath and President Richard Nixon held high-level meetings in Bermuda in December of 1971. Other problems were on the agenda, but the Irish problem was plaguing Heath mightily then. No more sympathetic listener than Richard Nixon could have been found. Long steeped in the mentality of ferreting out subversives, cast in the self-appointed role of defender of the American-Gothic order, terrorist hunts were Dick Nixon's *raison d'etre.* From California Commies to Potomac "pinkoes," he had harried them all. It had made his career. He would chase the Irish underground with relish. So the orders went out from on high, from the man who in his visit to Ireland, could find no politically useful relatives in Timahoe, County Limerick graveyards. The campaign was on. Foreign Minister of the Irish Republic, Patrick Hillery, met with Secretary of State William P. Rogers on February 3, 1972, and stated the case for caution with respect to Ulster. Dublin officials made it clear that the Republic was also very nervous about the IRA, and anything the United States could do to clip the wings of American supporters would be appreciated.

The pursuit of the Irish partisans was not without its zany aspects. In September, 1971, Joe Cahill, 51 year old Belfast IRA officer, was detained in New York when his visa was revoked. Cahill had been issued the visa prior to his previous visit to the United States in November, 1970. His return to America coincided with a bombing campaign in Belfast that blew up the Unionist Party headquarters and other offices there. Frank Durkan, Irish-born lawyer for Cahill and a member of the law firm of New York political leader Paul O'Dwyer, protested the government seizure of Cahill.

Durkan claimed Cahill's visa had been revoked by the Immigration and Naturalization Service while his client was in midair. A State Department spokesman said Cahill was seized on "information made available by the British government."[1] Irish partisans ground their teeth over their pints.

In another case, Charles Farrell Malone of the Irish Defense Committee of San Francisco was indicted by a grand jury on charges of shipping weapons to Ireland. Malone pleaded guilty, and Judge Samuel Conti suspended his one-year sentence, but placed Malone on a two-year probation. The strange feature of the case was that the judge urged Malone to forget he was Irish. He actually made it a provision of the probation that Malone stay out of Irish pubs and join no "Irish Catholic club." To amnesia was to be added a harsh abstention. "No speeches, no meetings, no farewell parties, and no Irish pubs," said Judge Conti. Such was the peculiar justice meted out to those snared by the Nixon administration's drive. In the period that spawned Watergate operations mixing old James Bond scripts and *opéra bouffe,* anything was possible.[2] The strange sentence imposed on Mr. Malone did not deter other San Francisco Irishmen, for in September 1973 Mr. Robert Meisel was jailed for contempt of court for refusing to testify before a grand jury. The twenty-six year old Viet Nam veteran was suspected of complicity in an arms smuggling plot. In Butte, Montana, and in St. Louis, in Buffalo and even in Miami among Cuban exiles, there were rumors of IRA gun deals. As one old-time partisan of the IRA put it, "If we had no law and I had the freedom to do it, I'd ship the whole U. S. arsenal over there."[3]

The Government agents scurrying around to discover arms plots were not entirely out on a wild goose chase. There was arms smuggling. Officials of the Irish Republic confiscated six suitcases at Cobh that had been sent from New York on the liner Queen Elizabeth 2. This discovery followed by only four days a confiscation in Amsterdam's airport of Czech-made arms that had been intended for Ireland. The agents of the United States Treasury's Firearms, Alcohol, and Tobacco Tax Division were empowered to frustrate arms shipments under the Federal gun control act of 1968. American pressure forced the IRA to go far afield for weapons. Early in 1973 the British were faced with attacks in six different Ulster locations by Russian-made rockets so hardware was certainly getting into the North from overseas. What drove the Irish militants into froths of fury was that the United States had become arms dealer for the world. Israel, Greece, Turkey and a bizarre chain of Latin tyrannies were all funneled arms with alacrity, but the IRA was excluded, presumably because it was not a favored faction. Other factions were assiduously supported by the CIA all over the globe, but the United States government was not willing to wink one eye for the Irish underground. The inconsistency was glaring. One does not have to be a friend of the IRA to stand in amazement before the conflicting welter of American policy contradictions. The United States aided Kurdish rebels and Chilean torturers—but the IRA was out. Some terrorists were apparently alright. Big wars with big civilian casualties as part of state policies were conscionable. Little wars with smaller death tolls were called terrorism, and approval depended upon who you were terrorizing.

The campaign of the Federal sleuths and eager government attorneys reached something of a crescendo of vindictiveness for the American IRA fans with the case of the Fort Worth Five. In June 1972 the Department of Justice, then under the direction of Attorney General Richard Kleindienst, issued subpoenas ordering five New York men to Texas to answer questions before a grand jury. This action was taken under the Omnibus Crime Control Act of 1970. It was a peculiar procedure to require men to journey 1400 miles from their homes to testify, but it was entirely in character for the Nixon administration that sent operatives in disguise to pillage offices of private citizens. The five men, Matty Reilly, Tom Laffey, Paschal Monahan, Dan Crawford, and Ken Tierney were all working class activists of Irish Northern Aid. Why they were singled out for exotic legal treatment was never clear. The government never charged them with any crime. They were hustled before a grand jury without counsel to face questions about matters that were not explicitly defined. Their predicament infuriated the Irish Northern Aid followers.[4]

The jailing of the five men for contempt of grand jury procedures halfway across the country from their homes alarmed even the hardened civil liberties professionals who had seen just about every abuse of rights the nation could produce. The American Civil Liberties Union, the Lawyers Committee for Civil Rights, and other groups alerted by the shrieks that emerged from the Irish militant community, took a studied interest in the case. The Irish organizations formed defense committees. Confinement of the men in Fort Worth meant that they were far from the areas where the Irish could easily organize sympathizers. They were almost incommunicado. Their families could not afford the expensive air fare to visit them. Judge Brewster, who was to hear their appeal, was widely known as a stern "hanging judge." The odds against the Fort Worth Five seemed a thousand to one in the face of government tactics.

Frank Durkan, the lawyer in the New York firm of Paul O'Dwyer, made the case his personal crusade, flying to Texas and rallying civil liberties organizations to aid in the defense. The Federal lawyers delayed the calling of witnesses so that the defendents languished in their cells. In May, 1972, Durkan, writing in the *Irish People,* contrasted the treatment of his clients with the protection and cover-up supplied to Watergate suspects. He compared the five Irishmen of modest status with the powerful men in high places mixed in the corruption of the Nixon administration. Indeed, Robert

Mardian of the Justice Department, who was the supposed architect of the anti-Irish campaign of the department, was widely known as the hatchet man for Attorney General John Mitchell, whose own career was crumbled in disgrace.

The Irish Northern Aid groups picketed Federal offices in a dozen cities, raised money to pay legal costs and support the families of the Fort Worth Five. They seethed at the legalistic railroading of the New York men. The case gave the American support network a needed symbol. Symbols of suffering and repression were numerous in Ireland. In the United States the Fort Worth Five provided a counterpart. The flagrant and abusive Federal handling of the case, so malicious legally, gave the Irish much needed allies in the liberal circles that had been alienated by the confusing strains of the Ulster problems and by the terror bombing in Ireland. For the Irish who had any attachment to or even sympathy for the support network, the Nixon administration became the most hated and reviled political regime since that of Herbert Hoover. It was almost as hated as the English, and that is a quantum hate.

Hated or not, the drive of the Federal agencies did not relent in vigilance. On February 14, 1974, the Federal bloodhounds finally sank their teeth into a case without a grand jury charade. Treasury agents arrested two men, James Conlon and Michael Larkin, in New York. It was alleged that they were part of a plot to smuggle $20,000 in arms purchased at a Maryland gun shop to Northern Ireland. The cache of one hundred AR-15 semi-automatic rifles was purchased in Kensington, Maryland. Three others, Kieran MacMahon, Harry Hillick, and William Westerfund were also arrested. Mr. Westerfund, the gun dealer, was released on his own recognizance as was Mr. MacMahon. The others were released on bail of $25,000, but Mr. Hillick, a citizen of Northern Ireland, was held on $200,000 bail. In April 1974 he went on a nine day hunger strike. A defense fund, The Irish American Legal Aid Fund, was set up in New York.

Frank Durkan, defender of the Fort Worth Five, took up the case for the four men charged with twenty-one counts of violation of law. Durkan told the court that his defendants "felt they should respond to a cry of help" for their brothers and sisters who were dying in Northern Ireland. The court was not impressed. The four men were sentenced in Baltimore on July 9, 1974 to six years each in prison.[5]

There is no way of telling how much more arms traffic there was that escaped government discovery. The men in the bars that were hangouts for IRA sympathizers would assure you that there was plenty. Certainly the shooting continued in Northern Ireland. As the violence in Ulster tapered off a bit in 1974, attention was focused however on grisly hunger strikes by two sisters, Dolours and Maria Price, held in prison in England on charges they took part in a bombing of London's downtown. The sisters were force-fed and came close to death before the Home Secretary altered their terms of confinement and they agreed to take food. Less fortunate was Michael Gaughan, an IRA recruit from County Mayo, who, despite brutal forced feeding, died on his hunger strike. Protests, picketing, and memorial services were held in various American cities in honor of the young martyr.[6]

The attempts of the Nixon administration to run the IRA supporters into the ground were typical of its hapless efforts in every direction. The subsequent revelations of FBI and CIA illegalities on a massive scale make it clear how easily government skullduggery can proliferate, and how casually and cynically law breakers and the innocent both can be railroaded. For those committed to the IRA, the Federal efforts increased their wariness and their alienation, and also gave them excellent propaganda material. For those opposed to the IRA the continuation of the support network beyond the Federal fumbling made that network seem all the more formidable.

Despite its evasion of the first round of the crackdown by Federal government agents and lawyers, the Irish activists had not been able to marshal strong blocs of American opinion to their cause. Despite all the picketing, propaganda, letter writing, and persistence of the committed cadre, they had not been able to enlist one major non-Irish American organization on their side. Groups working in the fields of foreign policy, interreligious understanding and anti-colonial concerns seemed to shun the Irish case. The civil liberties groups, it is true, had rallied to the support of the Fort Worth Five, but this was the sole example of American organizational alliance outside the Irish community itself.

This organizational isolation is traceable to various factors. The United States State Department and higher government circles were largely inhabited by men without ties to the Irish immigrant community. The Ivy League and power broker careerists in Washington simply didn't know anything or give a damn about Northern Ireland. They did care about England and its requests and suggestions to the United States. England was an important ally. Nor were the Irish of much domestic political significance. Their old power had declined. They had attached to them a dual political image, that of old time ward boss vulgarity, typified by Mayor Edward Daly of Chicago, and the Kennedy family drama of pain and disillusionment. Either part of the image was distressing to think about, and there was no longer any clear demographic and electoral Irish bloc of national significance to compel consideration of Irish concerns. In addition, the IRA supporters did not represent a broad base of adherents even among Irish-Americans.

Even more potent, however, were those two major characteristics of the Irish conflict itself, convoluted complexity and raging violence. The media coverage of the Ulster situation had opened the subject to international view, but the stereotypes and compressed accounts of the mass media simply created a need for more information. That information was not forthcoming in the media. Some organizations tried in a very small way to provide the information that would reveal the true complexity of the Northern Ireland situation. Lynne Shivers and Brad Lyttle, who worked with Quaker groups in Ulster, set up the Northern Ireland Information Service in Philadelphia. Their fact sheets, slide presentations, and speaking engagements were far too limited to tell the whole story. Their fact sheets, listing twenty-three major groups active in Ulster politics and strife and describing work for peace in the Six Counties, were not the kind of thing that newscasters or city room editors were going to present to the public.

The media concentration on violence emphasized the other chief characteristic inherent in the Northern problem, and the civilian toll and grisly murders in Ulster deepened the revulsion of Americans who may have started out with a sympathy for the nationalists in 1969. By 1974 when innocent tourists were blasted by explosives planted in the Tower of London and when the Houses of Parliament were bombed, Americans without the strongest Irish ties were fed up with the random death-deeds of the bombers. Although America has had a violent history, most Americans are not seriously conscious of this fact. The last war on American soil was in the 1860s. The bombing of civilians in Ireland produced the same sort of horror among conservative Americans as did the arms flaunting of the radical "Symbionese Liberation Army." Americans are selective about what violence they will tolerate, and the Irish variety turned them off.

The editors of the *Irish People* were conscious of the need to counteract this alienation of opinion and to give support to the thesis that the Provos were not engaging in barbarity. Dr. Fred Burns O'Brien of Washington D. C. contributed articles to the paper attempting to provide a reasoned ethical defense of Provo tactics. In 1973 Dr. O'Brien asked safeguards of human rights for people seized in the Irish Republic. After the bombing of the British Embassy in Washington, he hinted that the explosion was an English deed blamed on the IRA. He decried the British White Paper and plan for a Northern Ireland Assembly in 1973, and the exclusion of Sinn Fein leader Ruairi O'Bradaigh from the United States by Federal officials. Dr. O'Brien alleged that the power-sharing scheme for Ulster ignored the fact that the Unionist majority refused to work with the minority group. Pointing out that the American Revolution was full of "terror" deeds and that the Cyprus EOKA and the Irgun Zvai Leumi violence were excused, he asserted that British assassination and bomb squads were active in Ulster according to the testimony of such repulsive figures as the Littlejohn brothers, who were alleged English provocateurs. These arguments did not reach most Irish-Americans. Even if they had, they were hardly adequate in the face of the civilian maiming in Ireland.[7]

The stalemate in Ireland following the massive strike of the Ulster Workers Council in 1974 either caused or coincided with a decrease in violence in the Six Counties. The violent image remained, the real thing declined. This meant that the energizing effect constant headlines had on the American support network waned. This had its impact, and the support network lost ground. In addition, it was almost five years since the North had exploded, and the Irish supporters had been at their tasks for the whole time. Resolution flagged. Turnouts diminished. Apathy reconquered the spirits of many. The Irish are an exuberant people, but no one can be exuberant all the time. For some agitation was a way of life woven into their family and social habits. They continued their activities just as they continued to eat, work, and walk. But the support and opinion that could be mobilized to picket, rally, collect funds, and present the Irish case was eroding.

In 1975 a truce of sorts was arranged when the Provisional IRA agreed to suspend violence if the British suspended their own repression and violence. It was an uneasy half-peace, punctuated by sectarian murders, but at least the scale of violence in Ulster decreased. After three and a half years of direct rule from London, England sponsored a constitutional election and a convention that was to try to frame some government for the area. The United Ulster Unionist coalition of combined loyalist political parties won 46 of 78 seats for the convention and clearly dominated the political front. The hard-line groups and Protestant para-military organizations, in turn, dominated the politicians. Nationalists found nothing new in elections returning loyalist majorities in a statelet designed for that express purpose. As constitutional talks deadlocked on the issue of whether Catholics or those other than Unionists could be accorded any real power in the proposed new governing system, the cycle of violence begun to recur. Members of a show band were murdered after a musical engagement near Lurgan in August 1975. By September it seemed clear that the constitutional effort had been a failure. Oliver Napier, leader of the moderate Alliance Party in Ulster said, "This province is on the verge of a total breakdown."[8] More people moved out of Ulster. Many of those who stayed bought camping trailers so that if the worst came they could flee to the countryside with their families.

In the United States the Irish Northern Aid group and its allies recognized some of the shortcomings of their recent years of work with the general public. It was decided that a sharper focus for their efforts was needed. This took the form of a unified attempt to influence political opinion in Washington. Sean Walsh, an attorney, became the executive director of the Irish National Caucus with offices at 1025 Connecticut Avenue in Washington, D. C. The Executive Council of the Caucus included the head of the International Longshoreman's Union, Teddy Gleason, Rev. Sean McManus, John Henning, Dr. Fred Burns O'Brien, with Brendan McCusker as national liaison officer. The Board of Governors included Bishop Thomas J. Drury, Paul O'Dwyer and Daniel Cahalane, the Philadelphian who had been imprisoned by Richard Nixon's Attorney General. As an outgrowth of a meeting in New York in September 1974 the Irish National Caucus was pledged to "establish Irish Freedom as an American moral issue through every possible legal avenue at our disposal." In its platform and publicity material the organization used many arguments similar to those advanced by the Provisional IRA.[9]

A publicity breakthrough for Irish Northern Aid was secured in 1975 when a figure of particular significance for the news media began to appear at the group's affairs. The actor Richard Harris appeared with his wife and the wife of Provo leader Daithi O'Conaill in Baltimore at an Irish Northern Aid gathering and at other similar affairs. The Limerick-born actor was certainly a personality with great public appeal, and his presence gave the Irish Northern Aid a morale boost.

In September 1975 Sean Cronin wrote in *The Irish Times*, "Since 1973 Congressional interest in Northern Ireland has diminished appreciably. Many Congressmen, including (Senator Edward) Kennedy have backed off from an issue that has become simply too hot to handle. Congressmen understand well the dictum that little political prestige is to be won from battling a cause that stimulates so much negative reaction from both domestic sources and from overseas."[10] The rejection of power sharing by Ulster Protestants had led to headlines like "Toward War in Ulster."[11] New York's Paul O'Dwyer told a group of Congressmen that the United States should attempt to mediate the Ulster crisis, or "the area will be in chaos and the militant majority, armed to the teeth, will descend on the minority to drive them to their death."[12] The Congressmen were not moved. The subsequent news of such outrages as the London bombing that almost killed Caroline Kennedy, the bombing of London restaurants, and finally the killing of five Catholics in South Armagh and the horrendous retaliatory killing of ten Protestant workers on a bus was hardly likely to change their position.[13]

While the support network was trying to develop more calculated goals with respect to American opinion, the original tactics of random challenge to pro-British news in American papers continued. When C. L. Sulzberger of the *New York Times* wrote one of his pompous columns datelined Lisburn, the English military headquarters in Northern Ireland, he earned a stinging letter of rebuke two days later from Mark Barrett of the American Committee for Ulster Justice. One American activist did not content himself with letter writing. William Joseph Quinn, a Californian, was convicted of IRA membership in Dublin and given a twelve month sentence after being acquitted of assaulting and imprisoning a policeman in Donegal.[14]

As the frightful murders and uncertainties in Northern Ireland continued,

Dr. Conor Cruise-O'Brien and other Dublin officials also continued to address the American public and warn them against supporting the IRA. At the 1975 session of the American Committee for Irish Studies at Stonehill College in Massachusetts, Dr. Cruise-O'Brien repeated this exhortation. His critique of the twentieth-century Irish patriotic tradition drew swift and eloquent rebuttals from actor Shay Duffin and from Dr. John Murphy of University College, Cork. When questioned about just who the people were who were supporting the IRA, Dr. Cruise-O'Brien replied that he really did not know. Thus, while Irish Northern Aid began to change its tactics in the United States and keep a keen watch on trembling Ulster, the government of the Republic of Ireland stuck with its broad rhetoric and continued to accuse addled Americans of supporting Irish guerrillas.[15]

Late in 1975 the English government formally ended internment without trial in Northern Ireland.[16] The disastrous policy begun in 1971 which had stimulated much more disorder than it prevented was formally abandoned, although few Irish nationalists would believe that the announcement would deter English troops from "lifting" suspects in the future. The policy had been applied with wholesale force to Catholics but not Protestants in the North. In the United States the Irish Northern Aid groups found their most effective fund raising appeal was in asserting the need for money to aid the families of those confined in prison camps by this policy. The official abandonment of internment somewhat diminished the strength of this appeal. It also opened the way again for the British to go after the Provo support network in America.

Shortly after the London announcement of the official end of internment, Prime Minister Harold Wilson told the Association of American Correspondents that "misguided American supporters" of the IRA were providing "most of the modern weapons now reaching the terrorists in Northern Ireland." He accused those contributing to the Irish Northern Aid of "financing murder." It was a strong attack.[17]

Almost simultaneously a front page article in the *New York Times* written by Bernard Weinraub extensively summarized the charges that Irish Northern Aid was an arms conduit. It said that "United States intelligence sources in Washington" believed that 75 percent of the money Irish Northern Aid collected had gone for arms. One of the heads of the Irish group, Matthew Higgins, an old IRA man, was quoted as saying that if money sent to Ireland was used for guns, "we have no objections to it if they have money to spare. They've got to get them somewhere."[18]

The long article in the *New York Times* impressed many people, but not supporters of Irish Northern Aid. They found little new in it that had not been publicized previously. The internment announcement, the address by Mr. Wilson, and the long article were seen as a one-two-three assault directly inspired by London strategists. They predicted more Federal activity, and their predictions seemed to have been borne out when Daniel Cahalane of Philadelphia and four others were indicted on gun smuggling charges dating back to 1970.[19] The IRA supporters noted that two of the three indicted were in Ireland in 1975 and the case seemed to be a warming up of old charges in response to London's renewed concern. They also circulated a clipping from the *Irish Times* telling of arms smuggling from Scotland to Protestant para-military groups in Ulster.[20] They emphasized that Mr. Wilson had not mentioned this arms traffic.

In reviewing the importance of the American support network for the nationalist campaign of agitation and insurrection in Northern Ireland, the broad outlines of what had happened in Ireland must be kept in mind. The historic rift with England had been again torn open after decades of quasi-settlement. The English mechanism for ruling Northern Ireland had been shattered and a military rule had been clamped on the province. The Irish insurgents had ridden the tide of local bitterness and established a strong underground in a short time, though their strategy and tactics in the North alienated important elements of potential support by terror bombing and organizational defaults. A critically needed support network for the Ulster guerrillas was developed in England and the United States. The American network functioned effectively, though relatively small and limited in its Irish-American following. It was not able to influence American policy and indeed fell afoul of United States government investigation and suppression. While it evaded federal attempts to break it up its efforts did decline. Nevertheless, it was the most successful Irish overseas organizational activity in decades, matching the Irish Republic's own diplomatic work in impact. The Irish support network in America not only sustained the very long tradition of trans-Atlantic Irish revolutionary dedication, it linked international radicalism once again to the Irish problem as in the days of the Fenian radicals of the 1860s. With the leverage of American supporters and funds, the rebels of the North once again thrust the problem of unfulfilled Irish development into historic prominence.

7

TOWARD RENEWAL

There is a strange ambiguity about exile groups and immigrant communities. They are mortgaged to the past, yet they have often advanced into a future not yet perceived in the old country. Inevitably the new host country deeply affects immigrant ties to the homeland. Movement from a less developed nation to one resounding with modern media and sophisticated technology causes conflicts in the immigrant. Usually, the immigrant bears in himself the love and memory of the native land where he spent his most impressionable years. Yet, he must seek a livelihood in a nation frequently hostile to the values he was taught to cherish. This has been true in the mid-twentieth century for immigrants from Ireland to the United States.

Some features of the reaction of those Irish in America who worked for the support network can be clearly traced to the American background. It was not only the Northern Ireland problem itself that produced the pipeline of funds for the Ulster militants. Factors in the American environment contributed to the phenomenon. The existence of little cells of Irish nationalist agitators in various cities provided the indispensible links for organization of a new underground in the 1970s. These small groups had hung on in spite of all the power of American influences to subvert small group activity not in harmony with contemporary trends. But, like the study of Hebrew, the celebration of Italian *feste,* and Chinese cooking, they survived as part of the ethnic subcultures that thread through American life. The remnants and memories of the Irish underground were the nodules around which the new network was constructed.

There is an important distinction concerning Irish nationalism that has been pointed out by Liam da Paor, whose book *Divided Ulster* is one of the best short treatments of the subject. He has noted that there are at least two main brands of Irish nationalism. One is derived from the eighteenth-century enlightenment and the libertarian thinking of the French Revolution. It is rational in its sources and rhetorical in its tradition. The other kind of Irish nationalism is what might be called "ethnic." It derives from direct socialization into cults of belief and patriotic tradition. It is the common Irishman's perception of and feeling for his people and their assertion of themselves. It is this "ethnic" nationalism that is the chief effusion of the support network for the Provisional IRA.

With respect to those who have given their efforts to this network, the interest that they have focused on it is in many ways magnified or distorted because of the fragmentary character of the Irish existence in the United States. Movement to America for most emigrants places them in a truncated relationship to their original culture. What exists in America is only a fragmentary reflection of the native place, a partial representation without the balancing context. Because it is partial, certain elements in the American representation become overemphasized. They become the measure of judgment to the exclusion of all else. Thus it is with "the patriot game." Irish nationalism is such a vivid and emotional feature of Irish life that it is not easily sublimated. For those emigrants away from Ireland it remains, indeed expands, as a focus of Irish identity. Counterbalancing considerations are lost in the distance. The concern for Ireland becomes emotionally generalized, and this corresponds well with nationalism, itself an emotional generalization.

Dr. Conor Cruise-O'Brien, the present Minister of Posts and Telegraphs in Dublin, has often decried the jingo-patriotism so common in Ireland. The Irish are certainly not alone in their indulgence of patriotic mythology. Indeed, they have perhaps a greater right to its flatteries and glorifications than most peoples. The trouble is not so much nationalist ideals and romance as the fact that the Irish people have been frustrated in their peaceful realization of the ideals, and have had to live with a long delayed revolution that fell far short of their needs and desires.

It is of significance, too, that because of the diversity and impersonality of American life, the Irish groups were left to pursue their militant agitation largely isolated from major American organizations. The attack on the movement by federal law enforcement agencies only served to reenforce the isolation. No major political or humanitarian organization conducted any dialog with the Irish partisans. The Catholic church disparaged its efforts repeatedly. The Irish activists were left in their own circuit, governed by their own traditional values, distrustful of the broader American scene that might have been expected to advert to their protests and cries of distress. To a degree, the success of the Irish support network was a symptom of the failure of America to take its minorities and their problems seriously.

The relentless quality of the violence, its apparent lack of a political goal, is seen by Hans Morganthau as a counterpart to the bankruptcy of policy on the part of the nation state. Such violence "is an act born not of political concern but of political frustration and despair. Unable to change the political order from within by the procedures made available by that political order, unable likewise to overthrow that political order through concerted acts of violence, that is revolution, the political activist finds in indiscriminate destruction a substitute for the meaningful political act." In Northern Ireland, however, there were not even means within the political order for its change.[1]

The many friends of Ireland in the United States who consciously avoided the network supporting the militants did so not because Dr. Patrick Hillary or Jack Lynch of the Republic or Prime Minister Harold Wilson of England urged them to do so. They avoided the network because they saw it as tied to more of the same murderous violence without solution that they recoiled from in Viet Nam. Many such people were closely connected to Ireland, but saw the militant struggle in the North as a no-win situation. Reviewing the literature of the violent years in the North, Jay Browne wrote that "everyone who writes of the hatred and violence of Northern Ireland and of the resultant destruction, agony and despair has certainly implied that the jeremiad will go terrifyingly on and on."[2] This recognition for Americans, with their special need for swift solutions to problems, cut deeply against the grain. It was apparent in 1969 to close students of the North that the Civil Rights movement forecast violence, and they recoiled from the plunge into the abyss.

Americans have more experience in balancing minority interests than they give themselves credit for, and the Irish-Americans have been a long time handily engaged in this pluralist art. The majority of them are quite practical enough to know that the one million Protestants in Northern Ireland are not going to dissolve and have to be dealt with ultimately in a political way. The more Ulster Protestants taste of the openness of American influence the better will be the prospects. Such influence will not be a major agent of change, but.it will help. England's input certainly has not helped, and London's bankruptcy is betokened by the Orwellian suggestion of Norman Macrae in *The Economist* (October 25, 1975) that a new view of citizen privacy must prevail in the future so that "out patient" treatment can control "irrational aggression." The world of narcotic government impends. Humans deserve better.

It is important to remember the diversity of Irish-American influence and opinion. Michael O'Sullivan, a photographer and journalist, went to Ireland and accompanied IRA Provisional guerrillas on their raids. He spoke with their leaders, lived with the IRA men of all ranks, and set down his reactions in a book of excellent photographs with a strongly Republican narrative. The text is Irish Catholic nationalism in full cry, replete with the poems and passionate tradition of the rebel partisans. It is whole-heartedly sympathetic to the Ulster Provisionals, and bears firsthand testimony to the author's involvement with them. Its references to the Irish past are extensive enough to surpass what most Irish-Americans would know of that past. Its gritty ardor for the rebels is of a quality beyond most Irish-Americans.[3] Michael O'Sullivan, however, is far from typical.

One American with a professional background in international studies expressed his views after an extended visit to Ireland in a different way:

> We assume, based on what we heard and read in Ireland, that as of the autumn of 1973 the Provisional IRA no longer had the active support of a large number of Irish people. . . the Provisional IRA had appropriated and was feeding on traditions older and broader than itself. In American terms, it would be called a "cultural rip-off."[4]

Such persons could not engage themselves with the militancy in Northern Ireland because they were not steeped in the hate that area distilled. Americans might share racism, ravaging vanity, and a tolerance for violence, but the Ulster codes of hate were different from their own codes.

In his reflective account of Irish-American reactions to "the old country's" problems, *I Am Of Ireland,* Richard Howard Brown tells of his visits to the island and his encounters with Provisional IRA partisans in the United States. The book is honest, naïve, sentimental, but it does provide an insight into a broad band of Irish-American perceptions of the Ulster tragedy. The author is a very competent executive, observant, reflective, and schooled in American values. He finds he is at a great social distance from the Irish of New York who support the Provos. They are narrowly committed, suspicious, and wounded by history. He is open, curious, and self-assured. The book, with its recollections of Irish visits and New York Irish groups, is a good calibration of Irish-American differences, and it reveals a good deal about why the IRA in the North of Ireland could not command stronger support in the United States.[5]

The level at which some educated Irish-American opinion could be engaged is indicated by some of the writings of Rev. Andrew Greeley, a Chicago sociologist and specialist in ethnic studies. Father Greeley makes clear his lack of sympathy with the IRA, but he strongly asserts that the guerrilla group was created by British repression in Ireland, revived by England's post-1969 terrorism and torture, and given support by the blind policies of London in Ulster. The argument of Father Greeley against colonialist stupidity would embrace United States Viet Nam policy and other examples of major power ruthlessness, and this argument would evince wide sympathy in Irish-American university and professional circles.[6]

The bloody muddle of neo-colonial tragedy in Ireland should encourage all who have good will toward that country to hope and work for a new future for the island. It is difficult to get people in Northern Ireland to agree that there is any promise for the future. They have been stricken and traduced time and again. It may be that some great leader will arise to lead the way out of sectarian and politically bigoted stalemate. Whatever the future, it is likely that Irish-Americans will take part in it, actually in a small way perhaps, but vicariously and sympathetically with the resonance of their own long tradition. It is not likely that the main impetus for Ireland's future will come from the United States, unless perhaps the Americans detect some bonanza of resources in or offshore Ireland. Barring such discovery, the forces shaping Ireland's future will be Irish, English, European. In what way will the Irish in the United States relate to that future?

If the Northern Ireland conflict continues, possibly even spreading, it is not beyond imagination that the American support network of the Northern militants could expand. An even more intense Irish struggle, one more generalized, could bring into active enlistment with the Irish militants a much broader representation of Irish-Americans. This would mean that a much more talented and widespread segment of people would be engaged. The Irish overseas network striving to subvert English interests would be much more difficult to counter. The potential for this kind of support is certainly extant in the United States. One has only to talk to Irish-Americans with ties to Ireland in the last three generations—and even further back—to learn of their belief in the central thesis of Irish nationalism: that England is a malignant influence upon the island's life.

If the conflict abates, if there is a gradual winding down of tension that permits some expedient government to work, then the grave task of social and economic reconstruction can be slowly begun. This effort is not likely to engage any appreciable segment of the Irish-American population, not because of any inherent restriction, but simply because there is no accessible medium for such engagement. The militant support network is largely negative in character. It was created to aid in fighting, not reconstruction. Americans with broader interest in Ireland than guerrilla resistance would hardly be aided in constructive concerns by the gun boys. Such Americans are without an effective agency for their interest. They range all the way from the people in Midwestern states who arranged to take Ulster children into their homes in 1973 as an international gesture of interreligious understanding, to people who have merely visited Ireland and liked it.[7] Serious students of Irish affairs, people with ties to Ireland who reject violence, Americans who are interested in developing nations generally, these have no real and broad vehicle to enable them to be of aid to the Ireland emerging beyond the violence and the current outmoded structures.

One influence that could significantly marshal Irish-American opinion and constructive assistance would be the government of the Republic of Ireland. But, this would require a much more active effort than anything that has emanated from the Irish Embassy or the consulates in the past. Diplomats are neither innovators nor organizers. They largely juggle known forces. The creative activity needed would have to be financed, led, and tended by special people with an enthusiasm for linking those related to Ireland overseas with the old country. This could be done both through high-level programs that would touch major American institutions and organizations, and more popular approaches that would bind emigrants and those of Irish ancestry to the country in more than a haphazard way. Study tours, educational and cultural exchange, development missions of many kinds, institutional matching schemes, fund drives, interreligious projects in social service, improved information services, and dozens of other possibilities exist and should be greatly increased. Peace in the North would still leave Ireland in a colonial shadow of economic disadvantages and cultural schism, but American interest could be focused on these problems.

Even though emigration to the United States might continue to decline, the Irish immigrant or long-term visitor in the United States is still a key element in the relations between the two countries. The Irish-American tie has persisted more on the basis of emigration than any other influence. In the future the emigrant to America or the long-term visitor is likely to have a much higher educational level than in the past. He or she will be much more oriented to urban values and managerial activities. The group will also include artists and cultural figures continuing the powerful cultural tradition of twentieth-century Ireland. The seeming absence of policy on the part of the Irish government for making more positive use of the Irish overseas as informal ambassadors would have to be changed if those in the United States were to play a more broadly constructive role than in the past.

The potential for American service to Ireland, aside from the obvious bonanza that tourism has proven to be, can be seen from a few examples. At the height of the bitter controversy over the January 1972 slayings of civilians in Derry, the International League for the Rights of Man requested an American law professor, Samuel Dash of Georgetown University, to study the report made by Lord Widgery on the role of the English army in the killings. Mr. Dash, later to become known for his work as Senate counsel in exposing the Watergate scandals, did a remarkable investigative work. His report leaves little doubt that the English government's self-exculpation in the Derry tragedy was the most callous political whitewash.[8] Again, Dr. Rona Fields, a psychologist, of the University of California, carried out careful research into the torture inflicted on internees in Northern Ireland. Her work made abundantly clear the calculated cruelty and heinous nature of the torture techniques applied, but repeatedly denied, by English officials.[9] Because they are Americans removed from direct involvement with the Ulster conflict, these two persons were able to add their evidence to public knowledge with special effect.

The work of Gary MacEoin provides another example. Mr. MacEoin, though Irish-born, has resided in the United States for decades. He has had very extensive experience in Latin America, but has retained a concern for life in Ireland. His book, *Northern Ireland: Captive of History* is probably the best presentation of background and analysis available on the subject, and it gains greatly by the American perspective MacEoin brings to it. Its liberality, objectivity, and especially its analysis of Irish Catholicism, is skillful and constructive.[10]

Father Christopher McCarthy is a Redemptionist priest, born in Ireland, but who has lived for years in America. Determined to help overcome the towering hatred in Ulster, he returned to the Clonard monastery in Belfast during the struggle. He made contact with Moral Re-Armament, a personalist movement for application of religious values. With funds gathered by Fred Small, a black New York longshoreman's union leader, he made a film presenting Catholic and Protestant people testifying to their unity for peace in Northern Ireland. In 1974 he brought the film and those who appeared in it to the United States and Canada to show that human trust could be maintained even in the violence of Ulster. His message was realistic and effective, though supporters of the militants contended that it left out the political problem that was the root of the Northern Ireland conflict.[11]

Wes Baker and Dave Bowman are clergymen, one a Presbyterian minister, and the other a Jesuit priest attached to the National Council of Churches in New York City. When the interreligious bitterness in Ulster was revealed these two men undertook a fact-finding tour of the violence-torn province. They returned to America convinced that more could be done for dialog across religious lines even amid terror. They met and kept in contact heroic people who have placed their lives in jeopardy repeatedly to sustain faith in humanity in murderous Belfast areas. Reverend Baker and Father Bowman have worked with various Irish church groups and peace organizations. They constructed a network called Friends of Reconciliation, and with a strong belief in the peaceful future of Ulster, they have continued to campaign for human sympathy, sanity, and social development. They have distributed lists of Ulster social work groups worthy of support. They have made repeated trips to Ireland to foster hope and to do whatever they were asked by residents of the North in the service of peace.[12]

In 1975 John McNelis, a business representative in Philadelphia, helped draft a statement about the violence in Ulster. He wanted to have the statement show that Irish people all over the world were deeply concerned about

the Ulster problem. He and others contacted people of Irish background
from Australia, Canada, Argentina, and in the United States. The following
statement, which the author also signed, resulted. It was initially signed
by a violinist for the Philadelphia Orchestra, a college teacher, a university
professor, and John McNelis:

An Open Letter on the Death of Children and Civilians in Ireland

We are people with bonds to Ireland. We share the Irish tradition though
our forebearers emigrated to other lands. Our families have shared, and
hopefully will continue to share, the goals and aspirations of the Irish nationalist struggle for independence and fulfillment. We have been gravely disturbed to repeatedly read of the tragedy and violence unleashed by conditions
in Northern Ireland. We have been shocked and saddened by the killing
and maiming of children and innocent civilians in the strife that has occurred
in Ireland and England. These deaths and these terrible injuries debase all
of the traditions represented in Ireland. They are accursed violations of
the true ideals of Irish nationalism, a ghastly mockery of English rule in
Northern Ireland, and a bitter indictment of poisonous influences in Irish
and English life.

It is not possible for those in other countries to lecture people in Ireland
about the armed expedients to which they have been driven by the conflicts
in Northern Ireland. Mob violence, armed defense of communities, military
occupation by thousands of troops, mass arrests, torture of prisoners, as-
sassinations and all manner of havoc have created conditions in which normal people would be driven to desperate measures. The sufferings of the
people in Northern Ireland have created a nightmare of repression that invites the contempt of ordinary men for those who have supposedly been
in charge of the institutions in that society. Certainly, England's role in
the area is subject to the most profound arraignment.

Those who use force in relation to Northern Ireland may do so because
of idealism, military doctrine, mental illness or even more incalculable motives. Whatever their motives, whatever their beliefs, the toll in life and
destruction, the deaths of children and the innocent, now cry out for a
restoration of humanity. Those who kill or torture must now ask themselves:
"Will any man believe that I seek or defend liberty when I come soaked in
so much blood?"

We recommend that in every city, town and village in Ireland that some
simple memorial be established to the children who have died as a result
of the violence since 1969. The memorial could be as simple as the print
of the hand of a child and a list of the children dead. Free of foreign inter-
ference, the Irish people should be left to look on such memorials, and
knowing this cost of political violence, plan the future of their island.

> Kathleen O'Carroll Dalschaert (Australia), musician
> Lucia Flynn Thomas (Argentina), teacher
> William Dunphy (Canada), teacher
> John McNelis (U. S.), executive

Such a statement could be signed by a great many Irish-Americans. Another Philadelphia executive drew up the following list for use among fraternal groups and such organizations as the World Affairs Council:

Ten Reasons Why Americans Should Be Concerned About Violence in Northern Ireland:

1. The troubles of humanity have a claim on all of us, but especially upon citizens of the richest and most powerful democracy in the world.
2. Ireland and the U. S. have had a historic tie in terms of population exchange and mutual interest in liberty.
3. Through visits to Ireland millions of Americans have seen the persistent poverty and problems inherited from past centuries of struggle. Such a small country as Ireland does not need more suffering.
4. The recent U. S. Immigration Act, effective in 1966, makes it much more difficult for immigrants from Ireland to enter this country. Those trapped in the slums of Belfast and Derry who might have emigrated have less hope than ever. We cannot ignore their plight.
5. Many U. S. companies now have plants and investments in Ireland. Some have fallen in with local patterns of religious discrimination. We should not overlook this.
6. We have seen the peril of problems long ignored in the Atlantic community. Cuba, Haiti, and Santo Domingo are examples. We cannot pretend that long-standing problems do not exist.
7. The NATO forces we equip are being used by the British Army in Northern Ireland. As taxpayers, we should be concerned about their use.
8. Britain has been involved in very explosive moves that could flare up into atomic wars. The Suez adventure was such a case. With a new navy in the Atlantic, Russia could increase interest in any trouble spot.
9. The children of Ulster are being bred in violence. Americans who give generously to the U. N. Children's Fund should not be idle while child minds are poisoned by hate.
10. One feature of the Ulster tragedy is that it is partly a religious antagonism. Religious people everywhere should be concerned to promote interfaith efforts to roll back bigotry.

The light of scholarship should shine impartially, and the need for it with respect to Northern Ireland is certainly clear. An American contribution to Irish studies has been made by Roger Hull, a legal scholar, whose book *The Irish Triangle: Conflict in Northern Ireland* was published in 1976. Hull was anxious to explore the constitutional and practical political problems represented by Northern Ireland. His book traces the tripartite interpretations of Ulster's position and tries to suggest some resolution to the conflicting political claims to the area. The author sees that the situation in recent years has brought an erosion of human rights in Ulster. He does not concede that the Republic of Ireland has a "legally defensible" claim to the Six Counties area partitioned since 1920. He does not see the IRA as having the legal status of a belligerent or even an insurrectionary force in international law. He does see England as continuing to have a "free rein" in the area.[13]

Mr. Hull's legal analysis leads him to look beyond the law for some resolution to the conflict. His book urges that England step aside and permit United Nations, mixed North Atlantic Treaty Organization, or European Economic Community forces to keep peace and guide reconstruction in the area. He views England's record as simply too bad to permit it further activity in charting Ulster's course. In addition, he urges England to look to American social developments to guide religious desegregation of Ulster's schools and community life. Mr. Hull's solution as proposed may be questionable for many, but his interest and scholarship are not.

One of the most thoughtful books written about the Ulster problem is a small volume produced by an American, Ronald Wells, a teacher at Calvin College, and an Englishman, Brian Mawhinney. The book is called *Conflict and Christianity in Northern Ireland* and was published in 1975. It is aimed at American readers, especially church-oriented ones. It provides the usual summary of the history of the problem, but goes on to make a shrewd and compassionate analysis of the difficulties of the Six Counties. The book offers a carefully reasoned critique of one of the few high level American statements on the situation in Northern Ireland, the article by Senator Edward Kennedy, "Ulster Is An International Issue" in *Foreign Policy* (Summer 1973). The authors disagree with Senator Kennedy's belief that only a unified Ireland can provide social justice for the North. Their disagreement is conscientious, civil, and hopeful. They make a strong plea for religious people to care about Ulster, though they stop short of advising Americans to involve themselves in the area in direct ways. Their book is a good example of a concerned American contribution to education about Ulster along the best lines of American principles of justice.[14]

The neglect by modern Ireland of the task of fostering effectively organized blocs of friends in such countries as the United States places Ireland at the peril of revolutionary cadres that do take international ties seriously. The lack of effective overseas organization is, of course, part of a historic Irish government failure to deal realistically with emigration. The movement of people, especially the young, away from Ireland is as much a socio-psychological phenomenon as one of economic necessity. It may be a problem too big for any government to deal with. But governments, such as that of Norway, can work to bind the emigrants to their native land in constructive ways, and can provide inducements for their return. Special arrangements for education of emigrants and their children, strong information services, special tax provisions, and pension inducements can all be helpful. Primarily the responsibility is one of seeing the Irish overseas as more than intermittent Aer Lingus freight or troublesome cousins.

The activities of Americans seeking to aid peaceful elements in Northern Ireland may seem to be of small consideration in the face of the death toll and destruction in Ulster. They may seem paltry in the light of the ancient antagonism and the brutalized political traditions prevailing there. The complexities of statecraft have, however, been contravened, and new directions have been determined, by initially limited events. A struggle about a farm in the wastes of County Mayo began the effective work of the Irish Land League that helped win the land from alien control. The backroom agitation of a wing of radicals precipitated the drive for an independent Irish state. It is impossible to know from what direction social and political inspiration will come. The work of reconciliation for Northern Ireland may begin with American inspiration, as the civil rights drive there did. The contributions cited above all have this extremely important feature, they are disinterested efforts that keep in focus the human costs and needs underlying any political designs or desires. This is a crucially important task. Politics must serve human needs. The sacrifice of these needs to guerrilla war or forced occupation is damnable and is an execrable perpetuation of the tradition of tragedy that has so cruelly stalked Irish history.

The work of the people cited in this chapter is thoughtful and sometimes professional. It is not simply emotional commitment to an anti-English tradition. This means that it is all but isolated from the level of Irish subcultural life in the United States from which the support network for the Provos was formed. What is necessary for the future is that these two kinds of social groupings be brought into dialog and cooperation. Those with natural ties to Ireland and those with cultivated ties should not be estranged. The media for interest in Ireland should be greatly broadened, and this should be pursued as a much more active policy by the government of the Republic, and even those who are skeptical, or indeed, opposed to that government.

Americans interested in the future of Ireland should be concerned not alone with the problems and thinking of Irish immigrants. The superpowers are much too casual in their relations to small nations, and America must be attentive to the cultural traits of such nations. We must take care not to be classed with those men scathingly indicted by poet Thomas Kinsella in his harrowing poem "Butcher's Dozen" composed to commemorate those killed in Derry by the British army on "Bloody Sunday," 1972:

> My curse on the cunning and the bland,
> On gentlemen who loot a land
> They do not care to understand;[15]

We must "care to understand."

There is to be framed in 1976 in Philadelphia, where the American nation was founded, a Declaration of Interdependence to match the Declaration of Independence. A document affirming the links among peoples would be a salutary thing. The reality of those ties, however, is a more difficult testimony to perceive, tend, and respect. If, as has been stated in this book, there is a strong and special bond between Americans and Ireland, the practical knots and particular strands of that bond must be sorted out. This means study, leadership, and the fostering of mutual understanding between people of good will on both sides of the Atlantic. The government, universities, national organizations, churches, and political groups require a much more effective dialog if they are to realize this understanding. The tragedy of Northern Ireland, while having a peculiar power because of its roots in history, cannot be allowed to dominate the future of Ireland or Irish-American attachments to Ireland. The future is our intelligence, our commitment to peace, the courage of our common humanity, and the hope that is Ireland's most desperate need.

NOTES

CHAPTER ONE

1. Frank McDermot, *Theobold Wolfe Tone* (London: Macmillan and Co., 1939), pp. 171-75;
Charles Gavan Duffy, *Young Ireland* (New York: D. Appleton and Co., 1881);
T. W. Moody (ed.), *The Fenian Movement* (Cork, Ireland: Mercier Press, 1968);
Conor Cruise O'Brien, *Parnell and His Party: 1880–1890* (Oxford, England: Clarendon Press, 1957);
Sean Cronin, *The McGarrity Papers* (Tralee, Ireland: The Anvil Press, 1972).
2. Thomas N. Brown, *Irish American Nationalism* (Philadelphia: J. B. Lippincott, 1966).
3. Oscar Handlin, *Boston's Immigrants* (New York: Atheneum, 1969), pp. 151-53.
Dennis Clark, *The Irish in Philadelphia* (Philadelphia: Temple University Press, 1974), pp. 106-25.
4. Ibid., pp. 3-23, and Joseph P. O'Grady, *How the Irish Became Americans* (New York: Twayne Publishers, 1973), pp. 22-25.
5. John Devoy, *Recollections of an Irish Rebel* (New York: Charles P. Young, 1929).
6. Dorothy Macardle, *The Irish Republic* (London: Corgi Books, 1968).
7. Arnold Schier, *Ireland and the American Emigration* (Minneapolis, Minn.: University of Minnesota Press, 1958), pp. 167-68.
8. Paul Jones, *The Irish Brigade* (New York: Luce Publishers, 1969).
9. Oliver O'Byrne, *Freedom to Ireland: The Art and Science of War for the People* (Boston: Peter Donohoe, 1853).
10. Cronin, *The McGarrity Papers*, pp. 15-16.
11. J. Bowyer-Bell, *The Secret Army: The IRA, 1916–74* (Cambridge, Mass.: MIT Press, 1970) pp. 25–26.

12. Charles Callan Tansill, *America and the Fight for Irish Freedom* (New York: Devin-Adair Co., 1957).
13. Cronin, *The McGarrity Papers,* pp. 160-78; Bowyer-Bell, *The Secret Army,* pp. 136.
14. Cronin, *The McGarrity Papers,* p. 162.
15. F. S. L. Lyons, *Ireland Since the Famine* (London: Weidenfeld and Nicolson, 1971), p. 580.
16. Bowyer-Bell, *The Secret Army,* pp. 289-311.
17. Lyons, *Ireland Since the Famine,* pp. 728-47.
18. Gary MacEoin, *Northern Ireland: Captive of History* (New York: Holt-Rinehart and Winston, 1974), pp. 71-74.
19. Andrew Greeley, *That Most Distressful Nation* (Chicago: Quadrangle Books, 1969),
     Nathan Glazer and Daniel Patrick Moynihan, *Beyond the Melting Pot* (Cambridge, Mass.: MIT Press, Second Edition, 1970).

CHAPTER TWO

1. O'Neill, Lord, *The Autobiography of Terence O'Neill* (London: Rupert Hart-Davis, 1972).
2. Eamonn McCann, *War and an Irish Town* (Middlesex, England: Penguin Books, Ltd., 1974), pp. 27–116.
3. Ibid., pp. 32-52.
4. Bowes Egan and Vincent McCormick, *Burntollet* (London: LRS Publishers, 1969).
5. These events and much of what follows in this chapter is presented in chronological summary in Richard W. Mansbach (ed.), *Northern Ireland: Half a Century of Partition* (New York: Facts on File, 1973), pp. 57-210.
6. J. Bowyer-Bell, *The Secret Army: The IRA, 1916–74* (Cambridge, Mass.: MIT Press, 1970), pp. 373-92.
7. Bernadette Devlin, *The Price of My Soul* (London: Pan Books, Ltd, 1969), pp. 186-187.
8. Rosita Sweetman, *On Your Knees* (London: Pan Books, Ltd, 1972), pp. 201-13.
9. Donald Akenson, *The United States and Ireland* (Cambridge, Mass.: Harvard University Press, 1973), pp. 244-46.
10. *New York Times,* April 19, 1972.
11. Gary MacEoin, *Northern Ireland: Captive of History* (New York: Holt-Rinehart and Winston, 1974), pp. 83-84.
     The work of such groups is related in stories in the *New York Times* for August 11 and 15, September 10, October 20, December 2, 1971; and February 1, 5, 6; July 1, 17, 3, August 8, September 23 and December 19, 1972.
12. *The Times* (London), October 24, 1971.
13. Robert Moss, *War for the Cities* (New York: Coward, McCann and Geoghagan, Inc., 1972). This book gives a view of the IRA growth, but underrates its community impact. The IRA bombing strategy was summarized in a United Press International story by Donal O'Higgins filed from Belfast, February 1, 1972. A view of the

guerrilla in a world perspective is provided by Walter Laquer, "Guerrillas and Terrorists," *Commentary*, Vol. 58, No. 4 (October, 1974), 40-48.

CHAPTER THREE

1. Rosemary Harris, *Prejudice and Tolerance in Ulster* (Manchester, England: University of Manchester Press, 1972).
2. Garret Fitzgerald, Minister for Foreign Affairs of the Republic of Ireland in 1974, was still advancing the line that support for the IRA was from a "misled" minority of Irish Americans. The *Irish People* (New York), October 19, 1974.
3. Pete Hamill, *Irrational Ravings* (New York: G. P. Putnam's Sons, 1971), and Jimmy Breslin, *World Without End, Amen* (New York: Viking Publishers, 1973).
4. For the impact in Ireland of the U. S. civil rights struggle, see Gary MacEoin, *Northern Ireland: Captive of History* (New York: Holt-Rinehart and Winston, 1974), p. 83. The National Broadcasting Company showing of the documentary "Suffer the Little Children" on January 11, 1972, had special impact.
5. See the chronology of statements in Richard W. Mansbach (ed.), *Northern Ireland: Half a Century of Partition* (New York: Facts on File, 1973).
6. Rev. David Bowman of the staff of the National Council of Churches in New York monitored such activity. Helen Campbell of Derry, Northern Ireland, pleaded movingly for Quaker support of peace efforts there in a visit to U. S. Friends meetings in October 1972.
7. Population figures are from the Ninth Census of the U. S., and the Nineteenth Census of the U. S.
8. Rev. Andrew Greeley, *That Most Distressful Nation* (Chicago: Quadrangle Books, 1972) contends that by the 1970s the Irish in the U. S. were a group with vanishing ethnic identity.
9. 1970 Census of Population, Subject Reports, National Origin and Language, Bureau of the Census, U. S. Department of Commerce, Washington, D. C., June 1973, Table 15.
10. The bulletins of the Irish Republican Information Service were hot material. The editor of the Republican newspaper *An Phoblacht* (The People) (Dublin) was jailed for fifteen months for merely possessing copies. The *Irish People* (New York), October 19, 1974.
11. The *Irish People* (New York), September 22, 1973 and October 20, 1973. Testimony of Mr. Thomas Enright before the Subcommittee on Europe of the U. S. House of Representatives in 1972 claimed 70 Irish Northern Aid chapters in the U. S. Hearings Before the Subcommittee on Europe of the Committee on Foreign Affairs, House of Representatives, Ninety Second Congress, Second Session, February 28, 29 and March 1, 1972, p. 185.
12. The *Irish People* (New York), October 20, 1973.
13. Interview with Mr. Colin Owens of Kent State University, May 3, 1974.

14. Interviews with Dr. Perry Curtis of Brown University, formerly at the University of California at Berkeley, and Mr. Sean O'Callaghan, lawyer, in 1971 and 1972 a resident of Boston.

15. One such organizer addressed a rally in Philadelphia in January 1973, where militants of various groups assembled. The *Evening Bulletin* (Philadelphia), January 27, 1973.

16. Mansbach (ed.), *Northern Ireland*, passim.

17. MacEoin, *Northern Ireland: Captive of History*, pp. 261-80.

18. Hearings Before the Subcommittee on Europe of the Committee on Foreign Affairs, op. cit., pp. 2, 46, 63, 113, 115, 221, 224, 226.

19. Mansbach (ed.), *Northern Ireland*, pp. 88-9, 144-45, 147, 160.

20. Hearings Before the Subcommittee on Europe of the Committee on Foreign Affairs, p. 164.

21. My estimate of financial support for Northern Ireland relief, agitation and weapons is entirely my own, and is based upon estimates of organizational resources in major U. S. cities. *Time* magazine (December 23, 1974) gives an estimate of the Dublin government that $5 million has gone to the North from sources in the U. S.

CHAPTER FOUR

1. The Irish Republican News Service produced news releases that, if found on a person in the Irish Republic, were sufficient in themselves to have the person imprisoned, even though he might be a newsman. The *Irish People*, October 19, 1974.

2. Advertisements in the *Irish People* and other Irish newspapers announced such gatherings regularly from 1969 onward.

3. Dennis Clark, *The Irish in Philadelphia* (Philadelphia: Temple University Press, 1974), passim. Many of the succeeding facts are based on direct observations by the author.

4. For examples of such coverage, see the *Evening Bulletin*, August 14, 1972, and July 25, 1973, and the *Daily News*, October 21, 1973.

5. Hearings before the Subcommittee on Europe of the Committee on Foreign Affairs, House of Representatives, February 28–29 and March 1, 1972, pp. 323-324.

6. The *Daily News*, January 10, 1972.

7. The *Irish People*, September 29, 1973.

8. Michael Mallowe, "My Life and Times with the IRA," *Philadelphia Magazine*, (March 1973) (Philadelphia). Also the *Evening Bulletin*, February 2, 1976 and the *Sunday Bulletin*, January 11, 1976.

9. The *Philadelphia Inquirer*, May 9, 1973.

10. The *Evening Bulletin*, February 14, 1972.

11. The *Evening Bulletin*, July 25, 1973.

12. The *Irish People*, December 2, 1972, January 27, 1973.

13. The *Daily News* (Philadelphia), May 21, 1973, and *Philadelphia Inquirer*, July 16, 1973.

14. The *Evening Bulletin*, May 9, 1973.

15. The *Philadelphia Inquirer*, July 27, 1973.

16. The *Evening Bulletin*, October 31, 1973.

CHAPTER FIVE

1. These interviews were conducted informally over a period from 1970 to 1975 and passages quoted were transcribed immediately following the conversations. Informants knew that I was interested in Irish affairs as a social historian, and were willing to discuss the Ulster situation at length.

CHAPTER SIX

1. *New York Times*, September 3, 1971.
2. Associated Press story by Bernard Hurwitz on the trial before Judge Samuel Conti. The *Irish People*, September 29, 1973.
3. *Time*, December 23, 1974.
    The National Council of Irish-Americans in Buffalo, New York attributed the lack of a United Nations inquiry into the Northern Ireland issue to English pressure on the U. S.: *The Irish News* (Belfast), June 8, 1974.
4. Information on the Fort Worth Five was derived from 1972 and 1973 issues of the *Irish People* and from an interview with Mr. Frank Durkan one of the attorneys for the men imprisoned.
5. *The Irish Echo*, April 27, 1974; *New York Times*, July 10, 1974.
6. *New York Times*, July 15, 1974.
7. The *Irish People*, January 20, September 22, December 1, 1973; February 2 and 23, March 9 and May 11, 1974.
8. *New York Times*, September 29, 1975.
9. The *Irish People*, July 19, 1975.
10. *The Irish Times*, September 8, 1975.
11. *New York Times*, September 12, 1975.
12. *New York Times*, October, 16, 1975.
13. *New York Times*, October 23, 1975 and January 6, 1976.
14. *The Irish Press*, May 15, 1975.
15. The writer was present at the exchange on this occasion.
16. *New York Times*, December 16, 1975.
17. Ibid., December 17, 1975.
18. Ibid., December 16, 1975.
19. Ibid., December 23, 1975. Daniel Cahalene was eventually convicted of illegal arms buying by Federal authorities.
20. *The Irish Times*, December 8, 1975.

CHAPTER SEVEN

1. Hans Morgenthau, "Decline of Democratic Government," *The New Republic* (November 9, 1974).
2. Dr. Jay Browne, West Chester State College, West Chester, Pa., "The Literature of Violence: The Writer in Northern Ireland," unpublished manuscript.
    Vincent Tierney, "The Civil Rights Movement in Northern Ireland: Stalking Horse for the IRA?" American Committee for Irish Studies Conference, Virginia Polytechnic Institute and State University, Blacksburg, Va., May 3, 1974.

3. M. O'Sullivan, *Patriot Graves: Resistance in Ireland* (Chicago: Follett Publishing Co., 1972).

4. Quote from a journal compiled by an Irish-American who prefers to remain anonymous "because I have relatives in daily jeopardy in the North."

5. Richard Howard Brown, *I Am of Ireland* (New York: Harper & Row, 1974).

6. *Philadelphia Inquirer*, January 23, 1974.

6A. This prospect is raised in Alvin Shuster, "The Torment of Ulster," *New York Times Magazine*, February 2, 1975.

7. *New York Times*, July 10, 1974.

8. Samuel Dash, *Justice Denied: A Challenge to Lord Widgery's Report on "Bloody Sunday"* (New York: The Defense and Education Fund of the International League for the Rights of Man, 1972).

9. At a time when England was strenuously trying to control information about Ulster the book by Dr. Rona Fields, *Society on the Run: A Psychology of Northern Ireland* was withdrawn from circulation. An English publishing house held publishing rights to it, but refused to continue with publication.

10. Gary MacEoin, *Northern Ireland: Captive of History* (New York: Holt, Rinehart and Winston, 1974).

11. Father McCarthy is known to the author, and these remarks are based on attendance at his gathering in Philadelphia.

12. Father Bowman and Rev. Baker circulate a newsletter from 475 Riverside Drive, New York City, New York.

13. Roger H. Hull, *The Irish Triangle: Conflict in Northern Ireland* (Princeton: Princeton University Press, 1976), pp. 119-21, 263-71.

14. Brian Mawhinney and Ronald Wells, *Conflict and Christianity in Northern Ireland*, (Grand Rapids, Michigan: William B. Erdmans Co., 1975).

15. Thomas Kinsella, *Butcher's Dozen* (Dublin: Peppercanister, Dolmen Press, 1972).

BIBLIOGRAPHY

NEWSPAPERS

The *Daily News* (Philadelphia)
The *Evening Bulletin* (Philadelphia)
The *Irish People* (New York)
The Irish Times (Dublin)
The Times (London)
The *Philadelphia Inquirer* (Philadelphia)

BOOKS

Akenson, Donald, *The United States and Ireland* (Cambridge, Massachusetts: Harvard University Press, 1973).

Barritt, Denis and Charles Carter, *The North of Ireland Problem* (London: Oxford University Press, 1962).

Beckett, J. C., *A Short History of Ireland,* (New York: Harper and Row, 1968).

Bond, James E., *The Rules of Riot: Internal Conflicts and the Law of War,* (Princeton, New Jersey, Princeton University Press, 1974).

Boulton, David, *The "UVF": An Anatomy of a Loyalist Rebellion,* (Dublin: Torc Books, 1973).

Bowyer-Bell, J., *The Secret Army: The IRA: 1916-1974,* (Cambridge, Mass.: MIT Press, 1970).

Boyd, Andrew, *Holy War in Belfast,* (Tralee, Ireland: Anvil Books, 1969).

Brown, Thomas N., *Irish-American Nationalism,* (Philadelphia: J. B. Lippincott Co, 1966).

Carson, William, *Ulster and the Irish Republic,* (Belfast: William Cleland, Ltd., 1956).

Clark, Dennis, *The Irish in Philadelphia*, (Philadelphia: Temple University Press, 1974).

Clutterbuck, Richard, *Protest and the Urban Guerrilla*, (New York: Abelard Schuman, 1973).

Coogan, Tim Pat, *The I. R. A.*, (New York: Praeger Publishers, 1970).

Cronin, Sean, *The McGarrity Papers*, (Tralee, Ireland: The Anvil Press, 1972).

Cruise-O'Brien, Conor, *States of Ireland*, (New York: Pantheon Books, 1972).

Dash, Samuel, *Justice Denied: A Challenge to Lord Widgery's Report on "Bloody Sunday,"* (New York: International League for the Rights of Man, 1972).

Devlin, Bernadette, *The Price of My Soul*, (London: Pan Books, Ltd., 1969).

Dillon, Martin and Denis Lehane, *Political Murder In Northern Ireland*, (Harmondsworth, England: Penguin Books, 1973).

Dudley-Edwards, Owen, *The Sins of Our Fathers*, (London; Gill and Macmillan, 1970).

Egan, Bowes, and Vincent McCormick, *Burntollet*, (London: LRS Publishers, 1969).

Elliot, R. S. P., and John Hickie, *Ulster: A Case Study in Conflict Theory*, (London: Longmans Group, Ltd., 1971).

Fitzgerald, Garret, *Toward a New Ireland*, (London: Charles Knight, 1972).

Fitzgibbon, Constantine, *The Red Hand: The Ulster Colony*, (New York: Doubleday and Company, 1972).

Gallagher, Frank, *The Indivisible Island*, (New York: Citadel Press, 1957).

Good, James W., *Irish Unionism*, (Port Washington, New York: Kennikat Press, 1970, originally 1920).

Greaves, G. Desmond, *The Irish Crisis*, (London: Lawrence and Wishart, 1972).

Gwynn, Denis, *The History of Partition*, (Dublin: Browne, and Nolen, 1950).

Hand, Geoffrey (Introduction), *Report of the Irish Boundary Commission*, (Shannon, Ireland: Irish University Press, 1969).

Hastings, Max, *Barricades in Belfast*, (New York: Taplinger, 1970).

Heslinga, Marcus, *The Irish Border as a Cultural Divide*, (Assen, Netherlands: Van Gorcum and Company, 1971).

Hezlet, Arthur, *The "B" Specials, A History of the Ulster Special Constabulary*, (London: Tom Stacey, 1973).

Hull, Roger H., *The Irish Triangle: Conflict in Northern Ireland* (Princeton: Princeton University Press, 1976).

Jackson, Harold, *The Two Irelands: The Problem of the Double Minority*, (London: The Minority Rights Group, 1972).

Kiely, Benedict, *Counties in Contention*, (Cork, Ireland: Mercier Press, 1945).

King, Clifford, *The Orange and the Green*, (London: MacDonald, 1965).

Longford, The Earl of, and Thomas P. O'Neill, *Eamon de Valera*, (Boston: Houghton-Mifflin, 1971).

Macardle, Alice, *The Irish Republic*, (London: Corgi Books, 1968).

Magee, John, *Northern Ireland: Crisis and Conflict*, (London: Routledge and Kegan Paul, 1974).

Manhatten, Avro, *Religious Terror in Ireland,* (London:Paravision Publications, 1969).

Mansbach, Richard W. (ed.), *Northern Ireland: Half a Century of Partition,* (New York: Facts on File, 1973).

Mansergh, Nicholas, *The Irish Question,* (London: Allen & Unwin, Ltd., 1965).

Mawhinney, Brian and Ronald Wells, *Conflict and Christianity in Northern Ireland,* (Grand Rapids, Michigan: William B. Erdmans Publishing Co., 1975).

McDowell, R. B., *The Irish Convention: 1917-1918,* (London: Routledge and Kegan Paul).

McGuire, Maria, *To Take Arms: My Year With the IRA Provisionals,* (New York: Viking, 1973).

Montgomery-Hyde, H., *Carson,* (London: Heinemann, 1953).

O'Neill, Terence, *Ulster at the Crossroad,* (London: Faber and Faber, 1969).

O'Sullivan, P. Michael, *Patriot Graves: Resistance In Ireland,* (Chicago: Follett Publishing Company, 1972).

Paor, Liam de, *Divided Ulster,* (Baltimore, Maryland: Penguin Books, 1970).

Riddell, Patrick, *Fire Over Ulster,* (London: Hamish Hamilton, 1970).

Rose, Richard, *Governing Without Concensus,* (Boston: Beacon Press, 1970).

Schmitt, David, *The Irony of Irish Democracy,* (Lexington, Massachusetts: D. C. Heath, 1973).

Shannon, William V., *The American Irish,* (New York: The Macmillan Company, 1963).

Stetler, Russell, *The Battle of Bogside,* (London: Sheed and Ward, 1970).

Tansill, Charles Callan, *America and the Fight For Irish Freedom,* (New York: Devin-Adair Company, 1957).

The Orange and the Green, A Quaker Study of Community Relations in Northern Ireland, Briggflats, Sedbergy, Yorkshire, England, 1969.

Wallace, Martin, *Drums and Guns: Revolution in Ulster,* (London: Paravision Publications, 1969).

Walsh, Brendan, *Religion and Demographic Behavior In Ireland,* (Dublin: The Economic and Social Research Institute, 1970).

Weed, R. Douglas, *Tonight They'll Kill a Catholic,* (Carol Stream, Illinois: Creation House, 1974).

Williams, T. D., (ed.), *The Irish Struggle,* (London: Routledge and Kegan Paul, 1966).

Wilson, Thomas (ed)., *Ulster Under Home Rule,* (London: Oxford University Press, 1955).

Younger, Coulton, *A State of Division,* (London: Muller Ltd., 1972).

INDEX

A

Amnesty International, 24, 33

B

Baker, Rev. Wesley, 79
Bell, J. Bowyer, 58–59
Bowman, Rev. David, 79
British army, 20–24
British government, 20–22, 38–39, 63, 71, 75
Brown, Richard Howard, 76
Buckley, Sen. James, 39

C

Cahill, Joe, 63
Cahalane, Daniel, 49–50, 62, 72
Carey, Rep. Hugh, 39
Civil rights (U. S.), 32, 65
Cruise–O'Brien, Conor, 71, 74

D

Dash, Samuel, 78
De Valera, Eamon, 5, 10–11
Devlin (McAlisky), Bernadette, 18–19, 23, 37, 39, 45, 60
Drury, Bishop Thomas J., 36, 70
Durkan, Frank, 65–66

F

Federal law enforcement agencies, 49, 52–72 passim.
Fields, Dr. Rona, 78
Fort Worth Five, 65

G

Greeley, Rev. Andrew, 76
Green, Rep. William, 46

H

Hull, Roger, 81

I

Internment, 20
Irish-American communities, 4–5, 12–13, 19, 22, 31–33,
    43, 51–52; militant activities, 34–36, 42–43, 47, 51
Irish Defense Committee, 64
Irish National Caucus, 69–70
Irish nationalism, 3–4, 74; in U. S., 5–9
Irish Northern Aid, 35–39, 43, 50, 66, 71–72
Irish Republic, 10, 19–20, 21, 24, 26, 51–52, 63, 75
Irish Republican Army, ties to civil rights movement, 16;
    early lack of organization (1969), 17; post–war campaign
    1950's), 11; Official branch, 36–37, 40, 60; Provisional
    (Provo) branch, 18, 21, 25, 35, 37, 40, 51, 64, 75–76;
    American support for, 55–76

K

Kennedy, Sen. Edward, 39, 48–49, 70, 82

Mc

Mc Carthy, Re. Christopher, 79
Mac Eoin, Gary, 79
Mc Garrity, Joseph, 10, 35
Mc Kinney, Jack, 44
Mc Millan, Billy, 45
Mc Nelis, John, 79

M

Maudling, Reginald, 20
Mawhinney, Brian, 82

Media, influence of, 22–23, 34, 36, 41, 46–49, 68, 70, 75
Moderate groups in Northern Ireland, 38, 68; in U. S.,
    15–16, 19, 22, 24, 76–83

N

Nixon, (Richard M.) administration, 38–39, 49, 62
Northern Ireland, government, 15, 21
Northern Ireland Civil Rights Association, 15–16, 19, 22, 44

O

O'Brien, Dr. Fred Burns, 68
O'Dwyer, Paul, 38, 49, 63, 65, 70
O'Neill, Capt. Terence, 15–16
O'Sullivan, Michael, 75
Ottinger, Rep. William, 38

P

Paisley, Rev. Ian, 15, 23, 37
Prejudice, 30, 60
Protestant–Catholic relations, in Northern Ireland, 10, 15,
    28, 30, 53–59; in U. S., 33–34, 79
Psychology of militants, 30–32, 51, 59, 60–61, 74, 77–78

Q

Quakers, 68

R

Ribicoff, Sen. Abraham, 39
Rogers, Secretary of State William P. , 39

T

Television and violence, 18, 22–23
Torture, 24, 33

V

Violence and socialization, 27–28, 51

W

Wells, Ronald, 82